THE PURPOSE OF LIFE

Answers To Life's Greatest Questions

Other Books by Phil Batchelor

Raising Parents: *Nine Powerful Principles*

Love is a Verb: *published by St Martins Press*

The Purpose of Life

Answers To Life's Greatest Questions

Find Peace, Hope, and Joy
In a Troubled World

Phil Batchelor

The Purpose of Life:
Answers To Life's Greatest Questions

Published by:
Danville Int'l Publishing Company, LLC.
PO Box 3213
Danville, California 94526
www.planofhappiness.net

ISBN 0-9748528-0-5

Library of Congress Control Number:
2004092708

Printed in the United States of America.

10 9 8 7 6 5 4 3 2 1

In memory of
Gina Martin

Acknowledgments

This book is a composite of true stories from the lives of many valiant men and women who graciously gave permission for their experiences to be used in this volume.

I also express deep appreciation to Denise Mason and Sara Hoffman for substantial assistance in the editorial process; Steve Farrell for his inspired and insightful suggestions; and Kim Larsen and David Freeman for their assistance in the production of this volume. I also thank my dear wife, Carolee Batchelor, for reading endless drafts of the manuscript.

I thank Dave Christensen for his early support and encouragement, Cheryl and Lauren Locey for their generous assistance, Jared Stone, Jeff Smith, and the many other people who spent time reading drafts of the final manuscript and offering valuable suggestions.

CONTENTS

Preface

The Purpose of Life

Answers To Life's Greatest Questions

——• •——

I can remember it like it happened this morning, although it was many years ago. Close to death, a wonderful young father suffering with leukemia was taken to the hospital for the last time. His wife, their beautiful little children, and many members of his family and friends had gathered around to say their last good-byes.

As we stood around his hospital bed, he raised his head and asked everyone to leave the room to allow him a few moments alone. We all began to file out when he called to me, "Would you please wait?" I returned to his bedside as the door was closed, and in the next few minutes he poured out his heart to me. Tears began to roll down his face as he said, "I am afraid to die!" Then he asked a series of very important questions: "Why do I have to die and not have a chance to raise my sweet little children and be with my dear wife? When I die, where will I go, and what will become of me? Can you tell me what I can expect?"

I could see the longing in his tear-stained eyes as he expressed his tender emotions. I reflected on my own life and the numerous times I had asked some of these very same questions. Yes, life at times seemed so difficult and unfair, yet I very much wanted to be able to tell him that everything would be okay, that he was about to find peace and comfort, and that he was going to a better place. Words alone seemed so inadequate to express the deep feelings I had come to know and trust during my life. We shared some very special moments together, then his wife and children returned to express their love and say their good-byes, and soon he was gone.

I thought how peculiar it is that we seek most earnestly for the answers to life's greatest questions when we are on death's doorstep. Why not bring that satisfaction and peace of mind into our lives sooner? Why not experience the benefits throughout our lives, not just at the end? I have asked myself the following questions many times during my life:

- Who am I?

- Where did I come from?

- What is my purpose for being here on earth?

- Why do I have to experience hardship and difficulties?

- How can I find happiness?

- Why do I need a savior?

- What happens when I die?

- What happens at the time of resurrection and judgment?

As I have journeyed through life, I have discovered that there are answers to these questions, answers that will bring meaning, direction, and order to life, as well as greater peace of mind and confidence. I have learned that we can know who we really are, why we are here on earth, and what lies ahead once we have completed our journey in this life. The quest to find answers to these questions will be your most important investment in this lifetime, one that can unveil the greatest truths ever revealed.

Chapter One

Who Am I?

—••—

*W*hen I was a little boy of about five years of age, I remember venturing out into the deep end of a community swimming pool and quickly finding myself in serious trouble since I did not know how to swim. A man standing by the side of the pool saw my plight, jumped into the water, and saved me from drowning.

Since that frightening day so many years ago, I have asked myself, why was I saved? As I think about that day, I wonder, was I spared because I was lucky enough to have a compassionate stranger standing close at hand, or was I the recipient of a helping hand from a caring God who came to my aid through this Good Samaritan?

During the years that followed that experience, I pondered the idea that if God is mindful of the sparrow that falls to the ground, then surely he must care about us as human beings. I thought the concept that God is mindful of us was lofty, even wonderful, and wanted to believe it; but how could I really be sure?

I could not see God or hear Him, so how was I supposed to ever know Him? If He wanted me to come to know Him, then how would He make Himself known unto me? I received an answer to this question in a very dramatic way one night, many years ago. I was a student attending college and was driving home for Thanksgiving break to see my mother. It was a very cold and foggy night. As the fog became thicker, the road began to curve, and I could not see more than a few feet in front of me. I was traveling in the fast lane of a divided highway under an overpass when, without warning, my car began to spin out of control. It spun around 180 degrees and ended up perched on a raised bank of dirt, facing the oncoming traffic.

Most of the car was sticking out into the fast lane. To my horror, I realized I was about to die. I heard the awful sound of the giant eighteen-wheeler that had been behind me in the fast lane coming around the turn in the thick fog, and I knew it would pulverize both me and my car before it could stop. Suddenly I found myself pleading with God to save my life. Then I jammed the car into reverse and slammed the accelerator to the floor, but was terrified to find that the car just sat motionless as the tires spun. The truck was bearing down on me like a locomotive. Then, in a nanosecond, I was astonished to see the truck flash past me.

The truck driver instantly saw my dilemma, pulled over, and put out flares to warn the other traffic of my precarious situation as I sat there helpless. The highway patrol was called and all the traffic stopped. Then a large highway patrol officer and the good Samaritan truck driver pushed my car off the embankment. Amazingly, my car did not receive so much as a scratch. I turned the car around and the highway patrol officer said, "You are one lucky guy! You can go now."

However, just as I was getting ready to leave, the truck driver approached me and said, "I want to tell you something. I have been traveling this freeway for years, and I always take the inside lane when I come around this curve because I think it is safer. But tonight something told me to move over into the slow lane." That evening many years ago on a cold and foggy freeway, I came to know in a very real way that God is real and will make Himself known to us. That experience increased my desire to understand and know more about the reality of God.

The Reality of God

Some time after the accident, I picked up the Bible and opened it to the first page of the Old Testament and read how God created the heavens and the earth; separated the land from the waters and the light from the dark; and placed grass, trees, seeds, and animals of every kind upon the earth; and when he had completed His work, He described it as being "good."

When I thought about it, the reality of God was everywhere present. All I had to do was just take a moment to look around and I could see the clearest evidence that this earth did not come into being by accident. This earth is in a carefully prescribed orbit as it revolves around the sun and moves through space. Its distance from the sun gives it just enough light and heat to sustain human life. If it were to stray just a little too close or too far from the sun, it would be consumed by fire or it would become a ball of ice. It is tilted on its axis at just the right angle to bring about the seasons, and it rotates to bring the needed intervals of light and darkness. Life on earth operates under the most amazing system of checks and balances, allowing it to perpetuate itself. Yes, it is easy to understand why the God of heaven described His creations as being "good."

I wondered who could examine the beauty of a delicate flower, the majesty of a snow-covered mountain range, the glimmering sheen of a gorgeous mountain lake, or the brilliance of a sunset without knowing that a kind and benevolent being has prepared this planet for us. As Ralph Waldo Emerson put it,

"All I have seen teaches me to trust the creator for all I have not seen."

Yes, an examination of nature provided evidence that God was real, and so I read further in the first chapter of Genesis and came to a wonderful discovery about the reality of God. *And God said, Let us make man in our image, after our likeness: and let them have dominion over the fish of the sea, and over the fowl of the air, and over the cattle, and over all the earth, and over every creeping thing that creepeth upon the earth. So God created man in his own image, in the image of God created he him; male and female created he them.* [1.1]

It is marvelous to realize that the Creator made us in His own image and likeness. This fact teaches us about God, and it also teaches us about ourselves. It helped me to learn that God is not an impersonal being that fills the immensity of space or a shapeless, formless entity, but is instead real and tangible. If we saw God, we would see Him as a being that is similar to us, at least in shape and form. This profound truth, that man was created in the image of God, made it much easier to consider developing a relationship with Him.

Children of God

I also believe that, if God created us to be like Himself, then He must have a high regard for us; otherwise, He could have made us like any of the countless other creatures that He placed on the earth, none of which are like Him. What a wonderful concept to consider, that the Creator of the universe has made us as His grand finale, the climax of His creations on this earth.

Our existence *does* matter to Him, as I discovered as a college student on that fateful night so many years ago.

I have often thought about our relationship with God and wondered about how close we can really be to the Creator of the Universe. Again, I found an answer to my question in the Bible. In the New Testament, an apostle named Paul discussed the nature of God with the people of Athens, who were philosophizing about whether or not God really did exist. After Paul observed their altar with the inscription, "TO THE UNKNOWN GOD," he said, *"Whom therefore ye ignorantly worship, him declare I unto you. God that made the world and all things therein, seeing that he is Lord of heaven and earth . . . And hath made of one blood all nations of men for to dwell on all the face of the earth . . . That they should seek the Lord, if haply they might feel after him, and find him . . .* **For we are also his offspring.**" [1.2]

Paul's marvelous teachings helped me to understand not only that God wants us to seek to know Him but also that we are His children.

How glorious it was to realize that, because I am a child of God, I could look to my Heavenly Father for guidance, assistance, protection, and comfort in the same way that an earthly child looks to his or her father. Once I came to believe that I am a child of God, it changed my entire outlook on life! It not only expanded and enlarged my concept of who I am, but it gave real meaning to my purpose for being here on earth.

I regard the opportunity of being a father a wonderful and sacred privilege, and although I have a great love for my children, I lack the wisdom and understanding to be as good a father as I would like to be. Therefore, it seems reasonable to me that if I, an imperfect father, can have great affection and concern for my children, then our Father in Heaven, who is a perfect father, can and does have perfect love for us, His children.

However, I did not fully appreciate the extent of the love that our Heavenly Father has for us until I had the opportunity of watching my five-year-old daughter one windy day. We were flying a kite at the end of the court in front of our house. After some effort we managed to get our kite high up into the sky. We held onto the string together for the first few minutes, and then she said, "Daddy, let me hold it myself." I said, "Okay, honey, but be sure and hold tightly to the string."

Almost as soon as she had control of the kite, a gust of wind came up and jerked the string out of her hands. We watched helplessly as the kite sailed up and out of sight. My little daughter was upset over her loss, but I assured her we would buy another kite sometime and suggested that we go inside.

I started to walk toward the house but soon realized that my little daughter was not with me. I retraced my steps and discovered that she was kneeling on the lawn in front of our house and was praying. I listened carefully to her little prayer, "Heavenly Father, please help me find my kite."

I did not want to do anything to hurt her faith, but I had no idea how to find the kite. We got into the car and I drove about three blocks to a green belt area that is surrounded by houses. I reasoned that if we had any chance of finding the kite, it would be in this area. We drove over there, got out of the car, and began to walk along the path through the open grassy areas. After we had been walking for a few minutes, we saw some boys playing ball. I had a feeling I should talk to them. We approached them and asked, "Have any of you seen a kite?" One of them responded, "Yes, I have, it is on the roof of that house. Do you want me to get it for you?" Before I could answer or think of injury, falls, or liability insurance, he jumped up on the fence and climbed up on the roof and retrieved the kite. He climbed down and handed it to her. We thanked him and headed home. Yes, our Heavenly Father loves us, cares about us as his children, and hears and answers our prayers. He knows when a small child pleads for help, and He is aware of when we are in trouble and need help.

It seemed completely reasonable to me that God has made us in His likeness and image because we are His offspring, or children: We are related to the Creator of the Universe, and we therefore have a divine heritage. This is why He asked us to address

Him as Father in Heaven. What a tremendous concept this is to realize that we are related to the wisest and most powerful person in the universe. What a confirming comfort to know that I am not the product of a biological chance occurrence or accidental cosmic creation, but I am a Child of God. He is my Father!

Is God Mindful of His Children?

It made sense to me that if we are His children, then our Father in Heaven would be "mindful" of us. This is pointed out by Jesus Christ in his Sermon on the Mount, a magnificent discourse found in the New Testament. As part of his dissertation, Matthew, a follower of Christ, records two rhetorical questions that Jesus Christ asks about our relationship to God. Prior to posing each of these questions, Jesus gives His listeners a context that leads them to the answers. *"Behold the fowls of the air: for they sow not, neither do they reap, nor gather into barns; yet your heavenly Father feedeth them. Are ye not much better than they? . . . Consider the lilies of the field, how they grow; they toil not, neither do they spin: And yet I say unto you, That even Solomon in all his glory was not arrayed like one of these. Wherefore, if God so clothe the grass of the field, which to day is, and to morrow is cast into the oven, shall he not much more clothe you, O ye of little faith?"* [1.3]

If God pays attention even to the grass of the field and the birds of the air, it makes sense that He is going to be concerned about those whom He has made in His own image. What is the value of grass or a sparrow compared to the worth of a newborn baby, who is the son or daughter of God?

These inspired words by King David give credence to our standing before God: *"When I consider thy heavens, the work of thy fingers, the moon and the stars, which thou hast ordained; What is man, that thou art mindful of him? . . . For thou hast made him a little lower than the angels, and hast crowned him with glory and honour."*[1.4]

Seeking After God

Paul explained to the people of Athens that He wants us, the children of God, to seek Him out, to "feel after Him and find Him." I have wondered why the Creator of the universe, with all He has to do, would want us to seek after Him. How could a God who is busy making planets, stars, or solar systems have time to pause and listen to us? Then it occurred to me, that maybe God feels that it is more important to pay attention to His children than to focus His full attention on other activities in His universe. As a parallel, I have thought about the busy father who pauses from his important work as the ultimate decision-maker in the merging of two multi-billion dollar corporations to spend time with his children. He is wise enough to realize that, even though his occupation gives him these huge responsibilities, his relationship with his children is ultimately more important.

I wondered what my relationship should be or could be with God. How close could I be to a Father who didn't even live on this earth? Did God really want to be close to me? What could I bring to the relationship that would really matter to Him? I reasoned that if God is a perfect parent, it is unlikely that he would place His children on this earth and then just abandon them to become spiritual orphans.

I felt that just knowing that we are children of God was not enough. I wanted to be able to communicate with Him and, more importantly, have Him communicate with me. I felt that the real benefit to being an heir to God is that He has the power to help me, which He has done in the past and would do so again if I asked. I gained an increased assurance that this was the case as I continued to read the words of Jesus Christ in the Sermon on the Mount in the seventh chapter of Matthew. "*Ask, and it shall be given you; seek, and ye shall find; knock, and it shall be opened unto you: For every one that asketh receiveth; And he that seeketh findeth; and to him that knocketh it shall be opened. Or what man is there of you, whom if his son ask bread, will he give him a stone? Or if he ask a fish, will he give him a serpent? If ye then, being evil, know how to give good gifts unto your children, how much more shall your Father which is in heaven give good things to them that ask him?*"[1.5]

It was encouraging to know that our Heavenly Father wants us to call upon Him, and He promises us He will answer us and "give good things to them that ask Him." When I prayed to my Heavenly Father for help, it was not like going to my earthly father who, even if he were willing to help, may not have had the ability to do so. In the case of asking my Heavenly Father, I reasoned that He not only wanted to help but He was also fully capable of granting whatever I asked.

In spite of the fact that I believed Father could and would help me, there have been times in my life when I tried to do things without going to my Father to ask for assistance. It reminds me of a story I heard many years ago about a small boy trying to move a very large rock from the area where he was playing. His father watched as he struggled and pushed and strained to try and move the rock. His father asked, "Are you using all your strength?" "Yes," replied the little boy as tears of frustration streamed down his face. "No, you are not," said the father. "You have not asked me to help."

In time, I came to know for myself that God would answer my prayers, and I developed the habit of praying every morning and every night and sometimes a dozen or more times a day, depending upon what I was facing at the time. I have prayed for such mundane items as assistance in conducting a difficult meeting, but I have also asked my Heavenly Father to save my life, as recounted in the experience mentioned earlier about the automobile accident.

What a change this made in my thinking. I was not alone and could call on my Father in Heaven to help me in time of need. At any time I could call out and ask, "Father, are you there?" and He would hear and answer my prayers. This is exactly what happened when I awoke one night and found that my heart was beating rapidly and I was having a great deal of trouble breathing. As I labored to try and catch my breath, a wave of panic swept over me and I wondered if I was going to suffocate. It was very dark and cold, and I felt completely alone. Then in the midst of my anxiety, it occurred to me that I was not really alone, for I could call upon my Heavenly Father and He would help me. I prayed with great earnestness for His help that night, and within a few minutes my petition was granted: My heart rate returned to normal and I could breathe freely again.

As a result of my many experiences in asking my Heavenly Father for help, I have come to know with absolute certainty that God hears and answers prayers. He loves us and wants to help us and will make Himself known to us as we seek after Him to bring the blessings of heaven into our lives.

Nothing else I have learned in this life brings such comfort, self-confidence, and peace of mind as knowing that I am a child of God. This knowledge gives me the confidence to take on anything that comes my way because I know that the God of the universe is also my Father, and that He will help me if I ask.

Actions:

❖ Appreciate and be thankful for the beauty, order and intricacy of the world we live in.

❖ Contemplate the fact that you are created in the likeness and image of God.

❖ Remember that you are a child of God and are related to the Creator of the Universe who wants you to call Him Father.

❖ Understand that your Father in Heaven cares about you and wants to help you.

❖ Bring the power of heaven into your life each day by calling upon Heavenly Father in prayer.

❖ Remember you are never alone as long as you invite Heavenly Father into your life.

Chapter Two

Where Did I Come From?

———••———

One of the most precious experiences in my life was to have been in the delivery room to see the birth of my children. I remember holding my little daughter seconds after she came into this world. This tiny little girl looked around the room like she was wondering where she was, silently surveying her new surroundings. Cradled in my arms, she held onto one of my fingers. I was in awe of this perfect little person who already seemed to have a personality of her own, and I could not help but wonder where she came from, so beautiful, so vibrant, so perfect.

Certainly this little girl must have had a start to life before she entered the womb. It made me wonder if it was possible that before we came to earth we lived with God. Is it possible that Heavenly Father is mindful of us and cares about us because we have been part of His family since long before this world was created?

In the Old Testament, God talks about knowing us even before our birth. When God called Jeremiah to be a prophet, Jeremiah argued, "*I cannot speak, I am a child.*" So, to give Jeremiah greater confidence, the Lord reminded him of their prior association by saying, "*Before I formed thee in the belly I knew thee: and before thou camest forth out of the womb I sanctified thee, and I ordained thee a prophet unto the nations.*"[2.1]

How could the Lord have sanctified and ordained Jeremiah before he was born, and how could the Lord have known Jeremiah before he came out of the womb unless Jeremiah spent time with God before he was born? It seemed clear to me that we must have lived with God before we came to earth.

The apostle Paul confirms this when he talks about God calling and choosing us before the world was even made. Paul said, "*According as he hath chosen us in him before the foundation of the world*"[2.2] He later added, "*. . . Who hath saved us, and called us with a holy calling . . . before the world began.*"[2.3] If God chose us before the world was even made, we must have had a prior association with Him.

God also asks Job, "*Where wast thou when I laid the foundations of the earth?... When the morning stars sang together, and all the sons of God shouted for joy?*"[2.4] I have wondered who these "sons of God" were that existed before the earth was created even as I have pondered the question of who was in the heavenly host that praised God during the birth of Jesus Christ as recorded by Luke: *"And suddenly there was with the angel a multitude of the heavenly host praising God, and saying, Glory to God in the highest, and on earth peace, good will toward men."*[2.5]

I believe that we not only lived with God before we came to earth, but we shouted for joy as we watched with approval the things he did to prepare the earth as an abode for us. I think many of us were there, singing praises with the heavenly host that greeted the birth of Jesus Christ, who would become the Savior of the world.

Were We Nurtured in a Heavenly Home Before We Came to Earth?

If we did live with Heavenly Father before we came to earth, what must it have been like? Did Father establish a heavenly home for us that was a delightful place of beauty and comfort? How did God, our perfect parent, treat us?

I thought about the best things that my earthly parents did to teach me and help me as I was growing up and realized that the parenting in my heavenly home would undoubtedly have surpassed, by far, even the best things I experienced on earth. Our Perfect Father must have been very loving, kind, just, patient, and compassionate as well as a wise and wonderful teacher. He must have known exactly what we needed and how to teach us. I wondered what He would have taught us. I assume He would have encouraged us to learn and progress, giving us opportunities that were difficult enough to challenge us yet not so difficult that we would have felt overwhelmed.

What would we have talked about and what kind of a relationship would we have developed with our Heavenly Father? I believe we would have come to deeply cherish Him as we experienced His overwhelming love and affection for us, and we would have grown to respect, honor, and revere this God whom we called "Father."

The Time Came to Leave Our Heavenly Home

When we had learned the things we needed to know, did our Heavenly Father plan for the day when we were to leave heaven and come to earth? I wondered why Father would want us to leave our heavenly home. Was it equivalent to what happens on earth when we grow up and leave home and learn to make our own way in the world? Did our Father explain to us that although we had grown, developed, and progressed under His watchful eye, we would now need to leave home if we were to continue our educational process?

He must have sent us knowing that in this new environment we would learn to make decisions that would allow us to gain experience, understanding, and knowledge, a chance that would not be possible if we remained in our heavenly home in the care of our Perfect Father.

Once we came to earth, why didn't we remember the wonderful times and experiences we must have had in our heavenly home? Why would our Heavenly Father block out the wealth of memories that we must have gained over eons of time? Father must have had a very good reason for not allowing us to retain the recollection of the godly environment in which we once lived.

And if we had asked, might our Father have responded,

"My child, when you go to earth you will not remember living here because I will place a veil of forgetfulness across your mind. Your earthly experience has been designed so that you can learn to walk by faith. Through your experiences on earth, you will learn what is necessary to live and be happy here, lessons that you could not learn with me in Heaven. This process will allow you to continue to grow in wisdom, understanding, and knowledge, and it will help you to build and refine your character."

It also occurred to me that if we were able to remember the glorious time we spent in the realms of God, it would be difficult for us to function outside of that environment. I cannot help but wonder if we did express the concern to Heavenly Father about how difficult we felt it would be to have to suspend the close and loving relationships we had in our heavenly home in order to come to earth. Did Father explain that the veil that blocks our memory of life with Him also helps keep heavenly homesickness from becoming unbearable?

The inspired words of William Wordsworth in his *"Ode Intimations of Immortality from Recollections of Early Childhood"* emphasize the fact that this life is not the beginning of our existence.

> *"Our birth is but a sleep and a forgetting;*
> *The Soul that rises with us, our life's Star,*
> *Hath had elsewhere its setting,*
> *And cometh from afar;*
> *Not in entire forgetfulness,*
> *And not in utter nakedness,*
> *But trailing clouds of glory do we come*
> *From God, who is our home."*

I have found that when I keep in mind my relationship with Heavenly Father, remembering that I am His child, I have the confidence to take on the challenges of life. When I remember to pray to my Father and ask Him for help with my problems, I can overcome discouragement, depression, and the sense of being overwhelmed. When I feel alone, unwanted, or at the end of my rope, I pray to my Father in Heaven and He blesses me with feelings of peace, warmth, and comfort. These feelings combined with the answers I can receive reaffirm my belief that our Heavenly Father not only is mindful of us as His children, but He also loves us deeply and is ready and willing to help us if we will but ask.

I have also learned that our Heavenly Father is the one dependable source of help that will never let us down or disappoint us. His love is unconditional. I know He will love us no matter what, even when it seems like no one else will. It is never too late to turn to our Father in Heaven and ask Him to help us make a success out of our lives, for Heavenly Father will never abandon His children.

It is only when we forget to call upon Him or we ignore His direction that we place ourselves in the position of becoming spiritual orphans; for when we ignore our Heavenly Father, we cut ourselves off from the power of God and the blessings of heaven. Our Father wants to continue the loving relationship He had with us before we came to earth, and if we will allow Him to be part of our life, we will feel His love.

Actions:

❖ Ponder the fact that you lived in a heavenly home with your Father in Heaven before you were born.

❖ Understand that you were nurtured and tutored by your loving Heavenly Father until it was time for you to come to earth.

❖ Consider the reality that you were sent to earth to continue to learn, progress, and grow by the choices you make.

❖ Contemplate the fact that your Father in Heaven blocked out the memory of your pre-earth life so that you can learn to walk by faith, as you make decisions that will mold and shape your character.

❖ Ask your loving Heavenly Father to help you to again feel the closeness to Him that you once cherished.

Chapter Three

What is My Purpose for Being Here on Earth?

—•—

I remember as a little boy lying in bed at night and wanting to talk to God. I had very little religious education when I was young, but I knew God existed, and I wanted to talk with Him. Somehow I did not need anyone to tell me to talk to God; I felt the desire to do it even as a child. I had enough child-like faith to believe that God would guide me and I did not have to try and figure everything out for myself.

Have you ever asked yourself, "What is my purpose for being here on earth?" And, if you did, were you able to satisfactorily answer this question? Perhaps some people who feel that life is a chance occurrence see little need to even consider this inquiry, much less answer it. Other people who see the wisdom, order, and beauty of God's creations may feel that it is very important to understand why our Heavenly Father placed us on earth, and they desire to know what He wants us to accomplish.

If we were to ask our Father in Heaven to tell us why He has sent us to this earth, what do you think He would say? I believe He would tell us that the world was organized and prepared as our home so that we would gain a physical body and have the opportunity to learn and grow into the kind of individuals that could return to live with Him again in a state of never-ending happiness.

However, I believe He would also say, "There are certain things you need to accomplish during your life in order to receive an inheritance of heavenly beauty and happiness and to allow me to welcome you back into my presence. I would like you to:

- Learn to discern between good and evil and make correct choices..
- Learn to keep the commandments and serve others.
- Learn to pray for direction and help."

As we examine each of these requirements, I think that we will find that what is asked of us in return for eternal peace and joy is well worth the effort. Let us look at each of these qualifying factors.

Learn to Discern Between Good and Evil and Make Correct Choices.

Father has placed us here on earth to learn, grow, and progress. The only question is whether or not we choose to live the kind of life that will allow us to return to Him.

Our life experiences are made up of the decisions we make every day. Every time we make a decision, we are also selecting the consequence that comes with that decision. Although our Heavenly Father gives us the freedom to choose what we will do, He does not give us the freedom to choose the resulting consequences that come as a result of our choices. As Harry Emerson Fosdick said,

"He who chooses the beginning of a road chooses the place it leads to."

So the logical question might be, "Where do I want my path in life to ultimately lead me?" I assume that most of us want it to lead us back to the presence of our Heavenly Father, where we will find eternal peace and happiness.

Our Father gives us the freedom to choose what we will think, feel, and do; and each time we choose, we are influencing the kind of individual we will become. If we continue to choose to do things that help lighten the burden of others or show compassion and love for those in need, we develop a character that is charitable and caring. On the other hand, if we are completely wrapped up in ourselves and are egotistical and self-centered, we are forging a character that may be devoid of love and compassion.

I think that our Father in Heaven placed us on earth to give us the opportunity to develop into the kind of person that not only wants to return to live with Him but is also possessed of a character that would feel *comfortable* in the presence of divine purity, kindness, and love. I don't think any of us would want to be in an environment where we didn't fit in as a result of our character traits being completely different from those of everyone else.

Life is a composite of thousands of decisions, some good and some not so good, each of which influences the kind of person we become. A number of years ago, I had the opportunity of getting to know a talented young man who came to work in the same organization in which I worked. He started life by making very wise choices. He worked, studied, and earned his way into a prestigious university. He graduated with honors and went to work for a respected national firm.

He courted and married a wonderful young lady, and they had several beautiful children. They were able to purchase a nice house and settle down as a happy family. And then, slowly, things began to change. He felt overly confident, to the point of becoming cocky and arrogant. This attitude influenced the choices he made, and he began a long, slow, downward spiral.

He made choices that violated his commitment to his wife; he felt his superior intelligence allowed him to make choices independent of the desires of his colleagues at work; he then began to experiment with drugs and, as a result, he lost his wife, children, employment, and home. A few years later, he died in disgrace in a state prison where he had been incarcerated for selling drugs.

This failed life experience provides one example of the cumulative impact that our decisions can have on us. My co-worker, who started out making so many wise decisions, followed them with a number of very unwise decisions that resulted in his forfeiting everything.

This bright, disciplined, and hard-working individual reached a point in his life where he stopped progressing and instead started to regress with each poor choice he made until he lost his integrity, honor, and good name. In the space of less than forty years, this man soared to the pinnacle of success and then plummeted to the depths of despair and failure.

Once we decide what we want in life, it is not as simple as making a one-time decision that takes care of the issue for the rest of our life. There are opposing forces of good and evil independent of us that attempt to influence the decisions we make in life. These forces are trying to pull us in opposite directions. On one side is our Father in Heaven offering long-lasting joy and peace if we will do His will; on the other side is

Satan offering the pleasures of the moment but ultimately delivering only unhappiness.

We read in the book of Revelation in the New Testament that this conflict between good and evil has been going on since the beginning of time. Satan rebelled against God while he was in heaven and sought to take away our ability to choose for ourselves. He wanted God to give him the power to force mankind to obey all of God's laws. However, Satan's plan could never have worked; for if we were not free to choose, there would be no growth, learning, or progress, and thus the purpose that God had in sending us to the earth could have never been accomplished.

John records Satan's rebellion in heaven as follows: *"And there was war in heaven: Michael and his angels fought against the dragon [Satan]; and the dragon fought and his angels. And prevailed not; neither was their place found any more in heaven. And the great dragon was cast out, that old serpent, called the Devil, and Satan, which deceiveth the whole world: he was cast out into the earth, and his angels were cast out with him."* [3.1]

Today Satan and the spirit children of our Father in Heaven who followed him were cast out of heaven down to earth, where they continue to fight against all that is virtuous, noble, and pure. These "angels" of the Devil seek the misery and downfall of all of us. And so the war between good and evil continues even today, and we must choose whom we will follow.

It doesn't take long before we recognize that Satan is extremely cunning. He will advertise that which is evil as good and will gradually lead us down the road of misery by enticing us to succumb to our evil desires and our selfishness. He will help us rationalize our way through life, convincing us that we should focus on ourselves and our own needs and wants, to the exclusion of all else. He wants us to focus our attention on the things of the world, seeking for worldly honors such as popularity, position, and power. His agenda is for us to become not only completely self-centered and selfish but also material-minded and domineering. He would like to subject each of us to his will and desires. He is a tireless worker who will use music, movies, the Internet, magazines, books, and any other enticing stratagem to sell his program of misery.

To help us combat these forces and to help guide us, our Heavenly Father has given each of us an internal moral compass. We are all born with a conscience, or the natural capacity to distinguish between right and wrong. It will allow us to pass judgment on our own conduct, either approving of or condemning it. It helps us to make correct choices if we pay attention to its promptings. However, if we continue to ignore its influence, our conscience will eventually fade until we lose the benefit of this wonderful gift.

In the New Testament, the apostle John relates the story of a woman who was taken in adultery. When her accusers ask Jesus Christ what should be done with her, he responds, *"He that is without sin among you, let him first cast a stone at her. . And they which heard it, being convicted by their own conscience, went out one by one."*[3.2] This experience shows how our conscience can guide our actions and influence our choices.

The consequences of not choosing correctly are captured in a statement made by a 16th century moralist named William Law:

"If you have not chosen the Kingdom of God first, it will in the end make no difference what you have chosen instead."

In other words, even if most of the activities we have chosen to be involved in during this life appear to be meritorious and worthwhile, if they ignore what God has asked us to do then we have forfeited the ultimate inheritance that was available to us.

In summary, I believe that we have been placed upon this earth to learn and grow by having to choose between good and evil. On the one side we have the Devil and his followers trying to tempt us to make wrong choices; and on the other side we have a loving Heavenly Father who is willing to help us and who has given us a conscience that serves as a guide to help us make correct decisions.

Learn to Keep the Commandments & Serve Others

Heavenly Father gives us commandments so we can know how to live a life that will be acceptable to Him and that will fulfill our purpose for being here on earth.

For thousands of years His prophets, or spokesmen, have been recording the commandments God has given to His children. They are included as part of the sacred writings we call the scriptures, which have been given to us so we can know what our Father wants us to do. It is important to know the truth, as the Savior taught in the New Testament as recorded by John: *"If ye continue in my word, then are ye my disciples indeed; And ye shall know the truth and the truth shall make you free."*[3.3] If we want to be free, we must know God's word and be willing to live it. God's word is given to us in the form of commandments that can protect us, help us, and make us free. For example, in the Old Testament, Moses, the individual whom God selected to be a prophet and teacher of the people, was given a set of laws for all to follow. They were called the Ten Commandments. These commandments were intended as a set of guidelines that would help us to serve Him, work together in harmony, show respect for one another, and avoid doing things that would offend or harm others.

In the New Testament, Jesus Christ summarizes all the laws we have been given in two great commandments: *"Thou shalt love the Lord thy God with all thy heart, and with all thy soul, and with all thy mind. This is the first and great commandment. And the second is like unto it, Thou shalt love thy neighbour as thyself."* [3.4] I believe that if we make it our practice to serve and love God and our fellowmen, and if we do the things Father has asked of us, we will not only fulfill our purpose for being here but we will also find great joy in this life and in the life to come.

Once we determine what our Father in Heaven wants us to do, it is essential that we continue to pursue a path of righteousness for the remainder of our lives, regardless of the bumps in the road. Choosing to be righteous does not mean we will never meet disappointments, hardships, or discouragement; but it does mean that if we continually try to do what is right, Heavenly Father will bless us. In the writings of Matthew in the New Testament, the Savior promises, " . . . *he that endureth to the end shall be saved."* [3.5]

The Old Testament contains a marvelous example of this promise. In the book of Genesis, we read of an individual named Joseph who chose to keep God's commandments despite his many trials. When he was seventeen years old, his brothers sold him for twenty pieces of silver to a passing caravan of merchants bound for Egypt.

When the caravan arrived in Egypt, Joseph was sold as a slave. In spite of the fact that he would spend the next 13 years as a slave, a servant, and a prisoner, he never complained to God but instead continued to live the commandments.

Even when he was imprisoned after his employer's wife tried to seduce him and then falsely charged him with attacking her, he remained faithful. And as is always the case when we do what our Heavenly Father asks, the Lord blessed Joseph. The scriptural account of Joseph states: *"But the Lord was with Joseph, and shewed him mercy, ... and that which he did, the Lord made it to prosper."* [3.6]

Joseph's life was a pattern for righteous living that all of us can learn from. He lived righteously, no matter the circumstances. He never complained, but called on his Heavenly Father for help. When things appeared to be hopeless and seemed to be getting worse, he never lost hope.

When Joseph was thirty years old, the Lord reached down and lifted him from the depth of a prison dungeon by helping him to interpret the Pharaoh's dream. This King of Egypt esteemed Joseph above all others because he knew Joseph had the power of God in his life. In the fortieth chapter of Genesis, we read, *"And Pharaoh said unto his servants, Can we find such a one as this is, a man in whom the Spirit of God is? And Pharaoh said unto Joseph, Forasmuch as God hath shewed thee all this, there is none so discreet and wise as thou art: Thou shalt be over my house, and according unto thy word shall all my people be ruled: only in the throne will I be greater than thou."* [3..7]

Because of his faithfulness, Joseph was blessed beyond anything he could ever have imagined, which I believe is symbolic of what our Father promises each of us if we will keep His commandments and remain faithful to the end.

If in this life we choose to give in to the temptations of he who seeks our destruction, we will reap heartache and sorrow, and we will be disappointed in the kind of person we become. But if we choose wisely by living the commandments of our Father and following the promptings of our conscience, we will grow in wisdom and knowledge and will build a character that is filled with integrity and honor. We will become individuals who will one day be able to stand in the presence of our Savior and hear him say, " . . . *Come ye blessed of my Father, inherit the kingdom prepared for you from the foundation of the world.*"[3.8] We will have achieved our ultimate purpose in life!

Learn to Pray for Direction and Help

I believe that our Father in Heaven sent us to earth so that we could learn to walk by faith and to become more like Him. Considering the challenges, trials, and struggles we all encounter in life, I think it is unlikely that any of us can achieve this goal without assistance from Heaven. Therefore, it is vital that we learn to call upon our Father in Heaven for help.

I think that sometimes in a world that focuses so much upon the importance of freedoms and rights with little or no mention of duties and obligations, it is easy to get into trouble. In fact, it is amazing that so many young people have adopted the thinking expressed in the motto: *"Do your own thing."* And this popular slogan brings to mind an interview I had some years ago with three young ladies who had embraced this philosophy and found themselves incarcerated in a juvenile detention facility. Each was about 12 or 13 years old, and each had come from a dysfunctional family. One was an alcoholic who stole to support her addiction, the second was incarcerated for shooting someone who had made fun of her, and the third became involved in criminal behavior after joining a gang that she had belonged to since she was eight years old. The common denominator shared by all three of these young women was that they did not have anyone to help or guide them, nor to care about them when they most needed help. So, they were "doing their own thing" without the wisdom or maturity to know what to do.

I wonder if this is not analogous to the situation that we all find ourselves in from time to time? We come to a fork in the road and we do not have the wisdom to know which way we should go.

There have been times when I have thought that what I wanted was better than what Father wanted for me. These are the times when I inevitably seemed to follow a path that either turned out to be a dead end or else led to disappointment and sorrow. Although my Father knew I was going astray at the time, He did not stop me but instead allowed me the freedom to learn from my mistakes. However, at any time during my misguided adventures that I have called upon Him for help, He has been there. I have found that my relationship with God is one relationship that I would be foolish to ignore, for I lack the wisdom to know what I should do at times.

I have found that Heavenly Father will not interfere with our freedom of choice and insert Himself into our lives unless invited; but He will pour down the blessings of heaven upon us if we will use that freedom of choice to make Him a part of our life.

Why would anyone knowingly cut themselves off from the greatest source of power and assistance anywhere? Why would we want to take on any of the great challenges in our life without inviting our Father in Heaven to help us? What can we do better on our own than we can do with an infusion of heavenly help?

When I was older and read the Bible, I learned that the gospel writers repeatedly emphasized the importance of prayer. For example, Mark records these encouraging words, *"Therefore I say unto you, What things soever ye desire, when ye pray, believe that ye receive them, and ye shall have them."*[3.9]

I know that prayer works, and I have not, nor do I ever, intend to go through a single day without asking for the power of heaven to help me. In spite of my many shortcomings and inadequacies, I have had thousands of my prayers answered, and I know without a doubt that I do not have to take on the challenges of life by myself. Our merciful and loving Father in Heaven does not expect us to be perfect before we can talk to Him; otherwise, none of us would ever be worthy to pray. He answers our petitions and blesses our lives even though we may feel unworthy to receive such gifts.

Consider how often we find ourselves at a fork in the road of life and do not know which way to go. At times like this, we must decide if we will ask Heavenly Father for help. Choosing to do things on our own reminds me of a picture that hung on my office wall for years. It showed two men straining to pull a large cart that was equipped with square wheels, while inside the cart they were struggling with was the means to lighten their burden—an entire cartload of round wheels. How often do we struggle to make progress without calling upon the power of heaven to smooth out the rocky road before us or at least to give us the strength to traverse it?

In the book of James in the New Testament, there is a wonderful statement that reminds me of God's willingness to bless our lives. He writes, "*If any of you lack wisdom, let him ask of God, that giveth to all men liberally, and upbraideth not; and it shall be given him.*"3.10 God instructs us to ask Him for help when we need it, and he will not scold us or be upset but instead will grant our petitions.

My gracious Father in Heaven has answered thousands of my prayers during my lifetime. He answers my prayers not because I am worthy of receiving an answer but because He is loving, gracious, and kind, and He wants to help each of His children.

During the many years that I have been praying, I have found that my prayers are most effective when I remember the following:

1. Heavenly Father asks us to pray to Him directly; He does not want us to go through anyone else. He employs no assistants, secretaries, or aides.

2. When we pray, we need to have faith that our loving Father will hear us and will answer our prayers.

3. We do not need to make an appointment to talk to Heavenly Father. We can pray anytime we want to talk with Him.

4. We can pray anywhere, whether we are kneeling beside our beds, driving down the road, sitting in a meeting, standing before a crowd, sitting in an emergency room of a hospital, or anywhere we happen to be.

5. We can pray out loud or quietly, without uttering a word.

6. We should speak from our hearts when we talk to Heavenly Father and not use memorized prayers.

7. We need to pour out the feelings of our heart and tell Him what we are thinking and feeling the same way we would talk to a dear friend or a beloved earthly parent.

8. After we talk to Heavenly Father, we should pause and listen for an answer. It will usually come in the form of feelings or impressions in our heart or as thoughts that come into our mind.

9. When we pray, we should address Heavenly Father, thank Him for what He has already given us, ask for what we need, and then close in the name of Jesus Christ.

Prayer is a matter of expressing the feelings of our heart to a sympathetic, loving, compassionate, and receptive Father. We can stumble down the rocky road of trial and error on our own, or we can be wise enough to be guided by Him who paved the path. If we continue to call upon our Father in Heaven, we will realize that we are never alone and we do not have to work our way through this life on our own.

Once I came to know that Heavenly Father loves us, is mindful of us, and hears and answers our prayers, I felt a greater desire to draw closer to Him and to understand what He wanted me to do with my life. I wanted to know what I was supposed to learn and accomplish before my time on this earth was over. I realized that He was not going to ask me to do anything that He would not qualify me to be able to accomplish. And perhaps one of the greatest discoveries of my life came when I realized that what my Father in Heaven wants for me is better than anything I could ever want for myself. I know that He knows everything and can make more out of my life than I can if I choose to let Him into my life. I know that if I want my Father to give me answers to my prayers, I must be willing to do what He asks of me. Only then will He help me to achieve my goals.

Actions:

❖ Make decisions throughout your life that will help you develop the kind of character that will feel comfortable in the presence of divine purity, kindness, and love.

❖ Learn to choose between opposing forces of good and evil by paying attention to the promptings and feelings that come from your internal moral compass known as your conscience.

❖ Find fulfillment in life by serving and loving God and your fellowman.

❖ Follow these four simple steps when you pray: Address your Heavenly Father, thank Him for your blessings, ask for the things you need, and end your prayers in the name of Jesus Christ.

❖ Pray by pouring out the feelings of your heart instead of relying on memorized prayers.

❖ Listen for answers to your prayers, which usually come in the form of feelings and impressions in your heart or thoughts that come into your mind.

❖ Feel free to pray any time of the day, whether you are driving down the road or kneeling beside your bed.

❖ Place a copy of the following saying on your bathroom mirror, refrigerator, or desk: *"If you have not first chosen the kingdom of God, it will in the end make no difference what you have chosen instead."*

Chapter Four

Do I Have to Experience Hardships and Difficulties?

—•—

I believe that even though our Father in Heaven wants each of us to find peace and joy in this life, He has placed us on earth to learn how to deal with hardships, discouragement, depression, and despair. All of us will experience sickness, pain, frustration, and disappointments of one type or another.

Some of us will be burdened with debilitating diseases, the heartache of losing a loved one, a broken marriage, economic difficulties, the inability to realize the fulfillment of our heart's desire, or the trauma of seeing a loved one pursue a course of self-destruction. I think it is fair to say that the one common dominator is that all of us will have difficulties and unpleasant things happen to us sometime in our lives.

How Will We Respond to Our Challenges?

I believe that all of us are required to suffer, but how we respond to suffering is completely up to us. One day while I was writing this chapter I had an appointment with my dentist to have three crowns replaced. I was sitting in the dentist's chair, thinking that I did not particularly find this experience to be very pleasurable, when suddenly a memory from by childhood came into my mind. When I was about six years old and living in Venezuela, I walked into a room in the back of our house and found that our housekeeper was sitting in a chair and the gardener was pulling her badly decayed teeth out with a pair of rusty pliers. As I thought about this, it made me realize how fortunate I was to have the privilege of being able to receive adequate dental care, something a large portion of the world's population did not have. My thinking changed, and gratitude replaced grumbling.

Suffering can be a strengthening experience, or it can be a destructive force in our lives. This was reinforced for me in a remarkable way by witnessing how the life-threatening challenges of a friend of mine named Gina changed her life. Gina and her husband were happily married and had three children. This is her story in her own words.

"One day I went to the doctor for a checkup, and after my appointment I went to work. Later in the day, my doctor called me and asked me to come back to his office. I told him I was in a car pool and could not do that. Then he said, 'Well I want you to know that you have breast cancer and must be operated on immediately'. I was shocked at this devastating news! I turned completely white and almost fainted, and when I hung up the phone I started to cry. Suddenly thoughts began to stream into my mind. I was going to die and my three children would not have a mother to care for them. I am not ready to go yet. Why me? Why did I get cancer? What good reason was there for me to have to die? It is not fair. What did I do to deserve this?   After all, I believe in God, pray every day, and attend church on Sundays.

"First I went into denial and thought this must be a mistake. Then I got angry and began to take it out on my family, for I had told the doctor that I suspected it for years and had brought it to his attention repeatedly during past check-ups. But he kept telling me there was nothing to worry about. Now he was saying I have had breast cancer for at least two years and so the required surgery will be very comprehensive.

"Then I went into the stage where I accepted the fact that I had cancer and must deal with it. I had to utilize all the medical resources at my disposal. I needed to prepare myself to undergo surgery.

"At the same time that I was preparing for surgery, I realized that I must take care of myself spiritually. Although I regularly attended church, my relationship with my Heavenly Father had become somewhat casual. Now I was afraid, and I pleaded with Him repeatedly to help me until finally I had a feeling come to me that He would be with me.

"My casual relationship with my Father in Heaven was replaced with a deeper sense of closeness and warmth toward Him. I could feel His presence with me. I did not realize how beautiful it is to love God, and I would never have experienced this love if I had not been in the valley of despair and made a concerted effort to call upon Him. I came to realize that no one could help me but my Father in Heaven.

"Two weeks to the day of the diagnosis, I underwent an extensive surgical procedure. For the three months following the surgery, I experienced terrible pain. The chemotherapy treatments were next, which caused me to suffer physically and emotionally as I fought nausea, lost all my hair, and felt my dignity was being violated.

"Finally, after about nine months from the date of my surgery, the doctors told me that I was stabilized and the cancer was arrested. During the next thirty-three-month period, things returned to a more normal pattern, and I noticed I began to be less dependent on my Father in Heaven and again became more casual about my relationship with Him.

"I continued to watch my diet and to go in for regular medical checkups, including having CAT scans and bone scans taken. Not long after undergoing one battery of tests, the doctor called me into his office and told me the cancer had now spread to my bones. I asked him what it meant, and he told me I had only about two years left to live.

"Once again, I broke down and cried and began to feel sorry for myself. But this only lasted for one day. Then my thinking began to change. I told my husband we needed to get closer to Heavenly Father, and I needed to prepare to go back to my heavenly home. I know that He has a plan for me, and I want to understand what it is. Whether I live for two years or twenty, it does not matter, as long as I do everything I can to prepare to meet Him when my time comes. I am no longer afraid to die because Father is in charge. I have stopped praying to change God's mind. Now I pray to know His will for me.

"My family now prays together everyday, we attend church as a family, and I love my husband and children deeply. Our marriage has never been happier. I am trying to build memories and have learned to live and enjoy the moment.

"I would not wish this upon my worst enemy, but I am glad it happened to me because it taught me to know my Father in Heaven and to love Him. But I hope He will let me stay around for a couple of more years."

I am in awe of how much this wonderful young mother learned from her trials and how she managed to overcome the terror of her trials. She grew emotionally, mentally, and spiritually, and she prepared herself to be able to handle anything that life could throw at her. And most importantly, she came to know and love Heavenly Father better, causing her love for her family and for life itself to deepen and grow. I do not believe these things would have happened if she had not been tested and tried.

Trials to Build and Bless our Lives

Since our Heavenly Father really loves us and wants us to find joy and success in life, why does He let these things happen to us? He definitely has the power to keep them from happening. As I contemplated this apparent contradiction, it occurred to me that the answer is found in Genesis when God cast our first parents, Adam and Eve, out of the Garden of Eden.

The Lord said to Adam, *"Because thou hast hearkened unto the voice of thy wife, and hast eaten of the tree, of which I commanded thee, saying, Thou shalt not eat of it: **cursed is the ground for thy sake**; in sorrow shalt thou eat of it all the days of thy life; Thorns also and thistles shall it bring forth to thee; and thou shalt eat the herb of the field; In the sweat of thy face shalt thou eat bread till thou return unto the ground."*[4.1]   I am sure we would all agree that our stay on this earth was not meant to be a life of ease, comfort, and relaxation. The earth is "cursed for our sake"—or for our benefit.

What would we be like if we never needed to struggle to overcome hurdles in this life? Would any of us push ourselves to learn or grow if everything were handed to us without any effort on our part? When do we grow the most: When we are experiencing comfort and ease, or when we are struggling to achieve a goal? When do we gain appreciation for what we have: When there is an overflowing abundance, or when we are struggling to make ends meet? When do we turn to our Father in Heaven for help: When all is well, or when we are in need?

I believe that the Lord requires us to earn a living "by the sweat of our brow" not as a punishment but as a way to help us. He placed us on earth and gave us the opportunity to struggle and overcome so that we might build our character, refine our virtues and characteristics, and become better and more capable people.

The apostle John tells us that the Lord chastens those he loves. If we overcome the struggles of life, he will invite us to be with him and our Heavenly Father when this life is over. John quotes the Savior as follows: *"As many as I love, I rebuke and chasten: be zealous therefore and repent . . . To him that overcometh will I grant to sit with me in my throne, even as I also overcame, and am set down with my Father in his throne."*[4.2] I believe the Lord tests us so that we have the opportunity to practice and prove our loyalty and love for Him.

How Many Trials Will I Have?

I believe that each of us comes into this life with a different set of strengths, skills, and abilities as well as a different set of things we each need to learn.

Some need to learn patience; others compassion, empathy, or unconditional love. I think that life on earth is given to us as a workshop where we can work on overcoming our deficiencies that keep us from being more like Jesus Christ. Our trials serve as classes where we can learn to deal with our shortcomings.

"Okay", you might say, "but just how much refinement will I be required to endure? I have not enjoyed some of these life experience classes that were designed to teach me humility, patience, or compassion. Why must I enroll in some of them again and again?"

I am truly amazed that a man once walked the earth who was so extraordinary that he never made a single mistake. He was not only more pure, virtuous, and honest than anyone else, but he was also more intelligent, wise, kind, caring, courageous, and compassionate than anyone who lived on the earth before him or who ever will live after him.

In fact, no matter what virtue you consider, Jesus Christ possessed a fuller measure of it than anyone else did. Yet in the scriptures, the apostle Paul tells us, *"Though he were a Son, yet learned he obedience by the things which he suffered."*[4.3] If even the Savior could learn from suffering, then I know why I need to endure pain, disappointment and hardships in life; for I have so very much more to learn.

How Much Will the Lord Require Me to Bear?

We might say, "I understand why each of us must have some trials in life, but how much does Heavenly Father expect us to be able to bear?" We never know how strong we can be or how much we can bear until we reach the valley of despair, where Satan tries to convince us that we are weak and worthless and that neither Heavenly Father nor anyone else has any use for us. He tells us that we will be under a cloud of depression and gloom forever and that we are helpless to do anything about it.

This is the time when we are really being tested. We must decide if we will believe Satan's lies, or if we will follow the Savior, forging ahead with the strength of the Father to overcome our obstacles. And when we remember that we are children of God and that he loves us and wants us to succeed, our self-confidence increases. Then we gain the assurance that we can handle our personal challenges, even those that are the hardest to bear, such as the loss of a loved one.

I also know that there is a limit to the amount we will be required to bear. The apostle Paul confirms that the Lord will not require us to bear any burden that is greater than we can bear: *"There hath no temptation taking you but God is faithful, who will not suffer you to be tempted above that ye are able; but will with the temptation also make a way to escape, that ye may be able to bear it."*[4.4] Our Heavenly Father knows what we can handle and will come to our assistance before we are overwhelmed if we will just ask for His help.

My mother married at an early age without the benefit of a college education, and when the oldest of the three children in our family was only nine years of age, my father died. During the years that followed, I watched her struggle to enter the job market in order to support our family. We lived in a dozen different houses and three states as she continually tried to improve our lot in life. Without assistance from any relatives, she worked and struggled and did her best to care for her family.

The more she worked and struggled, the more she grew until she had gained a level of strength and independence that would never have been possible if my father had lived. My brother, sister, and I also learned how to work and accept responsibilities at an early age because of my father's passing. It is often the trials that we like the least that help us grow the most.

The Hardships We Bring Upon Ourselves

Sometimes we must wake up and realize that the unpleasant situation we find ourselves in is a direct result of our own actions and could have been avoided if we had made different choices. Frequently we bring upon ourselves the disappointments, hardships, and burdens we carry in life. Some of these problems could have been avoided if we had made different choices. For example, I wonder if my father would have died from lung cancer if he had not been such a heavy smoker. Would he have been able to live to see his family grow up?

However, it is a fact of life that we will all make mistakes, so we should try to learn from them and move on, doing our best to not make the same mistakes again.

The Hardships that Come to Us Naturally

Those who ignore or go against the teachings of our Father in Heaven will always have trials. However, there is also another reason we have trials and challenges—to accomplish the Lord's purposes for us. Sometimes when we sincerely pray for relief from pain or illness, to overcome loneliness, for the return of a wayward child, or to keep a loved one from slipping away, we may wonder why our heartfelt petitions are not granted.

If all our prayers were immediately answered, we could not grow. When our trials are not the consequence of our own misdeeds, then we can take some solace in the fact that our Father in Heaven is trying us and giving us opportunities to grow. He feels that we need to progress to a higher level of refinement. In the book of Proverbs in the Old Testament, the Lord explains: *"My son, despise not the*

chastening of the Lord; neither be weary of his correction:
For whom the Lord loved he corrected; even as a father the
son in whom he delighteth. "[4.5]

If we face our challenges by asking, "Why me?" or
"What did I do to deserve this?" we will become
frustrated, angry, and depressed as we are fighting
against the will of God. But if we ask, "What am I to
learn from this?" or "How can I change?" then we are
preparing ourselves to receive assistance from our
loving Heavenly Father.

Consider the wisdom of Gina, the wonderful young
mother mentioned above who, when she was dying of
cancer, said, "I have stopped praying to change God's
mind. Now I pray to know His will for me."

If we learn to trust in the Lord, we will realize that
He would not have us endure difficulty for even a
moment more than is absolutely necessary for our
personal welfare. Concerning this matter, the book of
Proverbs also gives us great counsel: *"Trust in the Lord*
with all thine heart; and lean not unto thine own
understanding. In all thy ways acknowledge him, and he
shall direct thy paths, Be not wise in thine own eyes: fear
the Lord, and depart from evil."[4.6] I know our Father
loves us and wants only the very best for us.

Learning From the Good Examples of Other People

I believe that sometimes the example of how other
people handle their burdens in life can inspire and

strengthen us. Such was the case of another friend of mine named Jan. She was possessed of a caring heart and an effervescent personality, and she was a friend to all who knew her.

She and her husband had two children and were a happy family. Then one day she returned home from the doctor's office with the news that she had cancer. Her friends questioned, "How could this happen to this wonderful young mother who has always done so much good?"

Jan went into the hospital for surgery, which was followed by a series of chemotherapy and radiation treatments. After all this, the best prognosis the doctors could offer her was they were hopeful that the cancer had been arrested. She was told not to have anymore children, for to do so would put her life in even greater jeopardy. But Jan refused to let her illness rule her life and eventually had two more children.

It was easy to know where Jan would be on any given day. All you had to do was to find a person who was in need, and she would be there helping, lifting, and encouraging. As the years went by, this wonderful lady continued to face more challenges.

One day she went in to check on her baby and was shocked to find that he was not breathing. He had died from SIDS. This was dreadful news for this tender and loving young mother to bear, but bear it she did and refused to be angry, to feel sorry for herself, or to become self-absorbed. She had an incredible amount of faith and love for her Father in Heaven, which allowed her to continue to be strong and to act instead of react.

The depth of her soul was then tested when, not long after the death of her son, Jan found that the cancer had returned. It was extraordinary to watch this noble soul increase in strength, courage, and compassion with every challenge.

At this point, Jan was spending a lot of time in the hospital. Whenever she went into the hospital, she was adamant that her husband tell no one. Nevertheless, sometimes the news would get out and people would come to visit her to bring words of comfort and cheer, only to discover as they left her hospital room that they had gained very little information about her condition.

As soon as her visitors arrived, she would turn the focus of the conversation around to talk about them and their state of well-being. By the time the visit ended, once again it was Jan who was nurturing instead of being nurtured.

This angelic lady continued her noble battle against her dreaded disease for twelve years. During this time she touched the lives of so many people. She lived her life in such an unselfish, positive, and cheerful way that she was an inspiration to all who knew her.

Jan dealt with the grief and pain in her life by first turning to Heavenly Father for help and then turning outward to bless the lives of others. She was an excellent role model on how to handle the misfortunes of life.

Be Still and Find a Refuge From Your Cares

We may say, "Well I am very grateful that our Heavenly Father loves us and cares about us and that someday I will be able to look back on this life and understand and appreciate it; but right now, life often seems so difficult and challenges never-ending. What can I do to find peace now?"

I have found that we do not have to wait until we die to find peace and tranquility in our troubled world. The apostle Paul tells us in the New Testament that our Heavenly Father will give us peace and joy. *"And the peace of God, which passeth all understanding, shall keep your hearts and minds through Christ Jesus."*[4.7]

I think that we too often lose sight of the fact that He has the power to help us through any trial. He who created the universe can certainly handle the problems that are so perplexing to us. If we try to carry the burdens of life on our backs without asking our Father for assistance, we encounter needless worry, frustration, and tension.

We need to learn to trust our Father in Heaven and believe Him when He tells us that, if we ask for help, He will do that which is best for us. We must learn to "be still" and know that He is God. As the Psalmist says, *"God is our refuge and strength, a very present help in trouble. Though the waters thereof roar and be troubled,*

*though the mountains shake with the swelling thereof. Be
still, and know that I am God."* [4.8]

When we quietly ponder, pray, and meditate, we
will be able to feel the warmth and love of our
Heavenly Father. We will come to know that we are
not alone. We do not have to face every difficulty and
hardship by ourselves. We can find peace in this life,
not just in the life to come.

Sometimes Our Trials Will Not Be Removed

I believe that there are times when we may pray for
relief from our trials without success. Sometimes we
find that our Father in Heaven wants us to endure
with patience our trials and learn from them. To me,
the best example of this is the experience of the apostle
Paul.

The scriptures tell us that he had a *"thorn in the
flesh,"* but we are not told what it was. Paul prayed
three times for it to be removed, and the Lord's
response was, *"My grace is sufficient for thee: for my
strength is made perfect in weakness."* [4.9]   Once Paul
received this answer from the Lord, his response was
amazing, *"Most gladly therefore will I rather glory in my
infirmities, that the power of Christ may rest upon me.
Therefore I take pleasure in infirmities, in reproaches, in
necessities in persecutions, in distresses for Christ's sake:
for when I am weak, then am I strong."* [4.10]

I believe that Paul's experience teaches us that if we
pray for relief from our burdens and Father does not

see fit to take our hardships from us, we should understand that He knows what is best for us, so we should do our best to carry on without complaint.

Perhaps it will be easier to get through the difficult times in our life when we keep in mind that the time we spend on earth is but one tick of the eternal clock in an unending eternity. We are here in mortality for a brief moment and then on to the next stage of our development.

It does not matter how many trials we have in life, just how we handle them. It does not matter how long we live, just how we live.

I have found that when I consider the answers to the following questions, it helps me to understand why we have trials and challenges in life.

- How can we appreciate eternal good health if we have never experienced sickness, pain, or disease?

- How can we appreciate eternal joy if we have never experienced disappointment, hardship, or failure?

- How can we appreciate living forever if we have never known death?

One of the reasons we were sent to earth is to encounter opposition. If there were no temptations, sickness, pain, disease, disappointments, hardships, failure or death in this life, it would be impossible to appreciate good health, happiness, or immortality in the life to come.

Our time on earth and the struggles of this life will give us appreciation for the glorious future our Father has prepared for us, making it possible to truly understand the significance of the eternal reward of the life hereafter.

Actions:

❖ Understand that you will experience hardships, disappointments, pain, frustration, and discouragement as a part of the learning process of earth life.

❖ Reflect on the fact that the greatest opportunities for growth and progress come during times of struggle and pain.

❖ Select a positive attitude that will allow your times of suffering to build you, not destroy you.

❖ Take comfort in the fact that your Heavenly Father will not require you to bear any burden that is greater than you can bear.

❖ Dwell on the opportunities that are left for you in this life, not on the mistakes of the past.

❖ Understand that if all our prayers were immediately answered, we would not grow and progress in this life.

❖ Avoid needless worry, frustration, and tension by turning to your Heavenly Father for comfort.

❖ It does not matter how many trials we have in life, just how we handle them. It does not matter how long we live, just how we live.

Chapter Five

Can I Find Happiness?

———•——

I believe that our kind and loving Heavenly Father wants each of us to live a life filled with happiness. It makes sense that a perfect Father would want His children to find happiness, just as we who are imperfect parents want our children to be happy. Happiness does not mean our lives will be free from difficulties; it has more to do with how we approach life despite the hardships. As the Psalmist in the Old Testament said, *"This is the day which the Lord hath made, we will rejoice and be glad in it."*[5.1]

You may ask, "How is it possible to find happiness in a world that is in commotion; that is filled with wars, terrorism, famine, floods, hurricanes, earthquakes, and endless accounts of man's inhumanity to man? If we are being realistic, is it still possible to be optimistic and happy in such an atmosphere of hatred and violence? I believe the answer is yes.

It seems that our happiness is not a function of the ebb and flow of world events, how much money we have, how good-looking we are, whether others are kind or fair to us, or even the state of our health. We have all known people who are in excellent health and possess every convenience available, yet they are still not happy. On the other hand, there are people who are racked with pain or who possess few of the things of the world who nevertheless always seem to have a good word for everyone and who are genuinely happy.

I like this statement that the famed author William James made:

"The greatest discovery of my lifetime was that a person can change the circumstances of his life by changing his thoughts and his attitudes."

It seems that a big factor that contributes to our state of happiness is the attitude we have about life.

We alone are responsible for the attitude we have about things. Our freedom to decide how we respond to life is dramatically pointed out in a marvelous little book by Viktor Frankl entitled *Man's Search for Meaning.* Mr. Frankl relates his experience in a Nazi concentration camp during World War II. While in this abhorrent environment where he was barbarically treated, Dr. Frankl makes an amazing discovery. He comes to the realization that although his body is incarcerated, his mind is not. He is free to mentally explore unlimited horizons. He need not fill his mind with thoughts of revenge and hatred or become so overcome by the detestable conditions that he gives up in despair. He, not his prison guards, determines his attitude. As a result, he becomes a symbol of hope and a positive rallying source for others in the concentration camp, helping many through this loathsome, inhumane test of endurance.

The attitude he has not only assists many of his fellow prisoners but also helps him mentally and emotionally. He learns that he is responsible for determining whether or not he will have a positive attitude; it is not a function of the circumstances he finds himself in during any particular hour of the day.

I also believe that our perspective in life is a critical factor in determining how happy we will be. Two individuals can be in the same set of circumstances, yet one is happy while the other is in deep despair.

For example, it is not uncommon to see news reporters interviewing people who have lost their houses and all their worldly possessions due to a natural disaster.

One family will bewail that they have lost everything they have worked for all their life and they do not know how they will go on. In contrast, another family will explain that, although they have lost all of their material possessions, they are so thankful to the Lord that they did not lose anything really important since their entire family is alive and well. Our perspective is key.

Recently I was talking to the parents of a family of seven children. When the conversation turned to the topic of family finances, the mother of the house admitted having some difficulties in making ends meet. But then she quickly added, "I am so glad that we are only talking about finances instead of worrying about something important like our health or the well-being of our children." If we do not stay focused, we will find that we can lose sight of what is really important. We will find ourselves looking only at the thorns in life instead of the roses.

This was clearly pointed out to me a number of years ago when I had the opportunity of speaking at the funeral of a special individual named Harold Willson. I liked being around Harold because he was an incredibly positive person and was always happy.

People would go out of their way to stop and talk with him because he would leave them feeling happy and upbeat. Harold was kind, considerate, and genuinely interested in people, and he treated everyone with respect. He maintained a cheerful disposition even though an accident at age twenty-one had left him paralyzed from the waist down.

Despite this misfortune, he refused to focus on what he could not do and instead focused his attention on the well-being of others. The important lesson I learned from Harold was that I can be happy in spite of the challenges life brings.

Happiness is not about being free of trouble, turmoil, illness, or worries. I believe that one of the reasons our Father placed us on this earth was to allow us to learn from the trials, hardships, disappointments, and misfortunes of life.

I think that one of the great realities of life is that we determine what will play upon the stage of our mind, whether it be comedy or tragedy. We can decide to look for the good in life, or we can agonize over that which did not go the way we wanted and stress about what the future might bring.

We can live in the sunlight of life or under clouds of gloom simply by deciding how happy we will be. I think Abraham Lincoln succinctly captured this same sentiment when he said,

"Most folks are about as happy as they make their minds up to be." (John Cook, The Book of Positive Quotations, 1997, p. 7)

When I find that I am not responding well to my circumstances or I am feeling sorry for myself, I can take action and change things. Some things that have helped me the most include the following:

Take time to listen to good music

❖ While I am driving, working, or just relaxing, I like to play music from the masters such as Beethoven,

Bach, Handel, Strauss, music from some of the great Broadway musicals; or inspirational gospel music. I find that listening to good music helps me overcome the blues and brings me feelings of encouragement and joy.

The Old Testament tells us that when Saul, the king of Israel, was troubled, he sent for David the shepherd boy to play for him: ". . . *David took an harp, and played with his hand: so Saul was refreshed, and was well.*"[5.2]

Maintain a sense of humor

❖ There is much to laugh about in life if we look for it. I believe it is imperative to not take ourselves too seriously and to learn to laugh at ourselves. A good sense of humor can relax tensions, reduce stress, and help bring peace into our lives.

Mark Twain, who had a wonderful sense of humor said,

"Humor is the great thing, the saving thing. The minute it crops up, all our irritations and resentments slip away, and a sunny spirit takes their place."

A number of years ago I remember a minister standing up in front of his congregation and saying, "I am certain that the Lord must have a sense of humor or he would not have made some of you people."

Be courteous and kind

❖ I have found that when I take steps to treat people with gentleness and kindness and seek to build their self-esteem, it makes me happier, and I feel better about myself.

I like the statement made by Jeremy Bentham,

"Kind words cost no more than unkind ones."

Not only does it not take any more effort to extend a word of kindness but it also invites a positive response from the recipient.

If we want to be around people who are positive and happy, why not be courteous and gracious? Then we can surround ourselves with those whom we have cheered rather than those who may be downcast or resentful. There are great opportunities to do good in this world that tends to celebrate the clever put downs.

Take time to smell the roses

❖ I have found much that is beautiful, lovely, and positive in this world, if I take time to notice it. As someone once said, "We generally find in life what we are looking for." Sometimes we overlook or take for granted the good things in life.

For example, I am sad that I did not take the time to really notice or appreciate flowers until I was in my fifties. Think of the many decades of beauty that were invisible to my unseeing eyes and the countless happy moments that might have been mine. I now try to savor the beauty of a sunset, the freshness of a spring day, and the brilliant wonder of a star-studded night sky; and when I do, it brings joy into my life.

Forget about yourself and serve others

❖ I once asked my teenage daughter how she believed people could find happiness in life and she said, "They need to stop thinking about themselves and help others." I believe she is correct. If you want a sure-fire formula for misery, spend your time and energy focusing on yourself. You will find that you spend all your time talking about your problems, worries, aches, and pains. You will make yourself and all around you miserable.

When I spend my time helping, lifting, and cheering others, I find that I am the principal beneficiary of my actions. It takes very little to brighten someone's day: a small note or card, a flower, a phone call, a listening ear, or a small gift can do wonders. I think it is a good rule to not retire for the night without first performing at least one small act of kindness for someone.

If these acts can sometimes be performed anonymously, so much the better. I believe that as we are comforting those who are sad, visiting the lonely, and helping those who are depressed or are needy, we will be making friends. They will reserve a place of affection in their hearts for us, and we will bring joy into their lives as well as our own.

There is a light-hearted poem written about how service can bring joy into our lives. I don't know who the author is. It is entitled,

How to be Happy.

"Are you almost disgusted with life, little man?
I'll tell you a wonderful trick
that will bring you contentment, if anything can,
Do something for somebody, quick!

Are you awfully tired with play, little girl?
Wearied, discouraged, and sick
I'll tell you the loveliest game in the world,
Do something for somebody, quick!

Though it rains like the rain of the flood, little man
and the clouds are forbidding and thick,
You can make the sun shine in your soul, little man,
Do something for somebody, quick!

Though the stars are like brass overhead, little girl,
and the walks like a well-heated brick
and our earthly affairs in a terrible whirl,
Do something for somebody, quick!"

Live in harmony with the laws of God

❖ I have found that no matter what else I do, I cannot find happiness if I am going against what my conscience says is right. I cannot do wrong and feel happy at the same time. If I ignore any of the ten commandments or choose to live only the ones I like, or if I break the "Golden Rule" and forget to treat people the way I want to be treated, I will not find peace or satisfaction, nor will I feel good about myself. As Abraham Lincoln said,

> *"When I do good, I feel good; when I do bad, I feel bad."*

I think that much of the turmoil in the world today is a result of so many people believing that they know what will bring happiness into their lives better than our Father in Heaven knows. They substitute their own judgment for the wisdom of our Heavenly Father, who knows everything, and the result is that we live in a troubled world.

The same course that can bring happiness and joy to us individually can bring peace and civility to the world if we all follow what our Father wants us to do. The most intelligent and wise person who ever lived upon this earth, Jesus Christ, lived by one unbreakable rule: He did only that which was his Father's will. I think if we could adopt this precept, it would bring a level of joy into our lives that would truly amaze us.

I have found that happiness comes into my life when I choose to be positive and happy, when I look for that which is good in life, and when I appreciate the many great blessings in my life. It seems easier to maintain a happy disposition when I listen to good music, have a sense of humor, show kindness to everyone, take time to smell the roses, forget about myself and serve others, and try to live my life in harmony with the laws of God. Is this enough? No, it is not! Then what is missing? If we are to be truly happy, we not only need a positive attitude and a willingness to act positively, but we must also have hope for the future.

How can we have hope for the future? Our hope comes from having faith in Jesus Christ and from knowing that he suffered, died, and was resurrected so that we might be forgiven of our sins. A more complete discussion of this topic will be provided in the next chapter.

We develop faith in Christ by experiencing a change of heart, so that we become meek and humble, and by taking upon ourselves the Christ-like qualities of love, compassion, and charity. When we are humble enough to do what our Father has asked us to do, then we will come to know true happiness.

Actions:

❖ Realize that you determine whether or not you will be happy, as you decide what will play upon the stage of your mind.

❖ Focus your attention on the roses in life, not the thorns.

❖ Recognize that happiness is not about being free of trouble, turmoil, illness, or worries.

❖ Listen to good music.

❖ Maintain a sense of humor.

❖ Be courteous and kind.

❖ Take time to smell the roses

❖ Forget about yourself and serve others.

❖ Live in harmony with the laws of God and follow the promptings of your conscience.

❖ Remember it does not matter how many trials we have in life, just how we handle them, or how long we live just how we live.

Chapter Six

Do I Need A Savior?

———•———

*T*he most important discovery of my life was to learn that we have a kind and loving Father in Heaven who loved us enough to send His Son, Jesus Christ, to save us from ourselves. There is nothing else I have learned or come to understand that in any way compares to this truth.

Our primary purpose in this life is to live in such a way that we can return to be with our Heavenly Father again. But because we are imperfect and have at times been unkind or selfish or have done other things we knew were wrong, we would not feel comfortable being in the presence of a perfect Father.

However, the good news is that our loving Father has provided a Savior who has done everything that is needed to help us to return to our heavenly home—*if* we will follow him. If we choose to follow him, we will find that our Savior, Jesus Christ, is the best friend we will ever have.

The Need for a Savior

The following story illustrates in a small way why the Savior is so important in my life:

One day you decide to go on a vacation that involves exploring an elaborate series of caves in a wilderness area. A dear friend who is a very experienced guide will be meeting you there. Once you arrive at your destination, you are so excited to start off on your adventure of exploring this mammoth series of caves that you don't wait for your friend but instead go on by yourself.

As you begin to explore the fascinating rock formations that make up the caves, you venture deeper and deeper into the dark caverns.

After some time you realize that your flashlight is very dim and is about to go out. Then suddenly it goes out and you find yourself in absolute darkness. You tell yourself not to panic, that you will be able to find your way out. Then you begin to think about the fact that there are some deep shafts in these caves and if you are not careful, you will fall into one of them.

You try to walk very carefully, feeling your way along the walls of the caves. But it is so dark that you have no idea which way to go or how you will ever get out of the caves. There are so many caves, and you realize that you are hopelessly lost. You think how grateful you would be if someone would come and guide you out of the darkness, gloom, and despair.

Then you see a light coming toward you. As it gets closer, you recognize your best friend, who is coming to your assistance. He explains to you what you need to do to keep from losing your life. Then he says, "Follow me," and leads you out of the darkness, keeping you from falling into the shafts or going in the wrong direction. As you make your way out of the darkness and once again feel the warmth of the sun on your face, you think how grateful you are to have such a wonderful friend.

Just as the guide in this story helped the unwise explorer find his way to safety, our friend, the Savior, will rescue us and show us the way to walk in this life if we will follow him. We find ourselves in the same situation in that we cannot return to our heavenly home alone. We need a guide to help us.

In the same way one might wonder what would have happened if there had been no guide in this story. I have asked myself, "What would have happened if our Father in Heaven had not provided a Savior for us?" What a horrible thought! Once we died, our bodies would remain forever in the grave. There would be no one to overcome death. We would have no hope of ever returning to live with our Father in Heaven. We would for eternity be subject to the harassment of Satan and his followers and would dwell in never-ending misery. I believe there is nothing more important for any of us than to have a Savior who can rescue us from death and from Satan.

A Savior Is Chosen

I can imagine what our Father in Heaven must have gone through so many years ago, before any of us came to earth, when He carefully selected the person who was to fill the role as the Savior of all mankind. Since our Father never forces us to do anything against our will, He must have asked who would be willing to step forward and volunteer to serve as the Messiah, or Savior of the world.

As an outstanding teacher, Heavenly Father must have explained that in order to qualify to serve as the Savior, the candidate would have to be willing and able to live a life absolutely free from sin; for were he to commit even one small error, he would not be eligible to be the pure and spotless sacrifice.

He would have to be willing to come to earth in the most humble of circumstances, to be born in a stable, and to grow up and live with very few of the things of the world. He would have to be loving and kind even in the face of harshness and cruelty, and he would have to be courageous enough to undergo the terrible tortures required to pay the price for everyone's sins.

I imagine that our Heavenly Father would have explained that the Savior would be required to:

- Serve as a perfect role model who would show us how to live so that we could return to our heavenly home.

- Teach us what we must do here on earth to one day be invited back into the presence of God.

- Undergo the most dreadful pain ever conceived in order to pay for the sins of all humanity.

- Overcome death, preparing the way for all of us to be able to live forever.

How grateful I am that there was one who could qualify to fill this role and who was willing to pay such an enormous price to save us. I am so thankful that Jesus Christ agreed to come to earth and live among men to do for us what we could not do for ourselves.

Jesus Christ, A Perfect Role Model

I think it is marvelous that Jesus Christ does not threaten or coerce us; but with kindness, gentleness, and love he says, "Come Follow Me." If we follow in his footsteps, he will *show* us the way to success and find happiness in this life and in the life to come.

When I trust in the Savior, he lights the way for me; but when I try to do things on my own, I stumble in the darkness. I have found that if I follow the example of the Savior, I can be more successful in anything I undertake in life. For example, most things in the world involve our ability to communicate with others.

If I follow the pattern that the Savior established, I will be kind, unselfish, compassionate, and forgiving; I will desire the welfare of all I meet and look for the good in others; I will not be judgmental nor seek to dominate others, but will instead be patient, gentle, and loving in my dealings with others.

One can learn more about human relations by studying the life and example of the Savior than he or she can learn by studying any book ever written on the subject. In fact, I believe you can select any of the virtues—honesty, love, courage, meekness, boldness, loyalty, charity, etc.—and you will find that the Savior possessed that virtue in fuller measure than anyone else who has ever lived on the earth.

If you were to develop each of these traits and virtues to the fullest, you would be like the Savior, the perfect role model. In a world that seems starved for role models, we have one ideal role model that will never disappoint us or let us down.

Jesus Christ, the Master Teacher

If I could sit at the feet of any teacher who ever lived, there is one person I would choose—Jesus Christ. In my opinion, there is no one else who is as intelligent and wise as the Savior. He brought the wisdom of heaven down to bless the lives of the children of God. He brought light to replace darkness, hope to overcome discouragement, knowledge to supersede ignorance, and peace to calm a troubled world. I believe a study of the teachings of the Savior can help us decide how to pursue any one of the infinite number of courses we could choose in this life.

As we study the tremendous sermons and teachings of Jesus Christ, we can grow in wisdom and knowledge; we can learn to use our time wisely and develop our talents, and we can find happiness in doing so. I know Jesus Christ will not only help us make the most out of our lives on earth but will also lead us back to our heavenly home so that we will have joy for the rest of eternity.

Jesus Christ Paid the Ransom Required to Rescue Us

It seems we are faced with a serious dilemma. Our Heavenly Father has placed us on earth to give us experience and to allow us to choose for ourselves whether we will return to live with Him. But in the process of learning through trial and error, we have all stumbled and fallen.

We have broken the commandments that we have been given. I believe that from time to time, we have decided that we wanted to do things our own way instead of the way our Father wants us to. I think we have relied upon our own wisdom instead of following the counsel of our God. And so we ask the question, "Have we disqualified ourselves from ever being able to return to our heavenly home, or is it possible that we can be rescued?"

The apostle Paul states, "*For all have sinned, and come short of the glory of God.*"[6.1] But since our Father in Heaven is perfect and will not tolerate sin in the least degree, how will any of us ever qualify to be with Him?

I don't believe our Father will forget about the commandments we broke or just ignore our errors out of love for us. I don't think He will tell us that, because He cares so much for us, it is okay for us to return to our heavenly home even though we have lived an unrighteous life. If He did, our Heavenly Father would not be a just God. He would lack credibility. Why would anyone bother to live His commandments or rules if there were no consequences for breaking them?

He has taught us that a price must be paid for the mistakes we have made, and Jesus Christ paid that price for those who repent and try to follow the commandments. I know that if we choose not to do our best to live the commandments and follow the Savior, we must suffer and pay for our own mistakes. But if we do our best, the Savior will stand as our defender and advocate.

Consider for a moment what it would be like if each of us were trapped in a burning building from which there was no escape. We know we cannot save ourselves, and unless someone comes to our rescue, we will surely die. The only one that has the ability to enter the burning building and endure the pain of the flames to rescue us is Jesus Christ.

The Savior knows our Father wants him to save us. However, in order to save each one of us, the Savior must endure additional pain. It is as if our Savior must repeatedly enter the burning building in which we are trapped in order to reach us and carry us out to safety.

In order to help us appreciate the reality of how the Savior paid for our mistakes, I like to travel back to the time when the Savior lived upon the earth and look at the greatest and yet most terrible events that have ever occurred in the history of the human race. Let us examine the price that was paid to free you and me from our sins.

It is Thursday evening, the last night Jesus Christ will spend on earth. We are in a small garden called Gethsemane on the Mount of Olives. Here a series of events is about to unfold that will change the world forever. What is to happen is critically important to us. The unthinkable is about to take place, for one man is about to take upon himself the sins and agonies of all the people who will ever live on the earth.

Jesus Christ is to take upon himself the full weight of all our misdeeds as well as the mistakes and sins of every other person who is part of the human family. He is the only one to live on the earth who is worthy to serve in this role. If he is unwilling or unable to do this, then there is no other person who can rescue us. But, oh, what a price he must pay! He not only takes on the suffering for our sins but also the burden of all of our illnesses, pains, sorrows, and disappointments.

As the Savior kneels to pray, the agony is so awful that it would bring death to any mortal being. Jesus must suffer that which could only be experienced by the Son of God. And he will not be allowed the merciful release from suffering that death brings, a release that you and I are given when we encounter too much pain.

He takes his chief apostles and closest friends — Peter, James, and John—with him to Gethsemane and asks them to be with him during this awful experience. But they provide little support to him as they fall asleep and, even after he wakes them, fall asleep again. This, the most difficult event in human history, the Savior must bear without the aid of any earthly companionship.

Luke records that he suffers so much that blood comes out of his pores: *"And being in an agony he prayed more earnestly; and his sweat was as it were great drops of blood falling down to the ground."*[6.2]

It is startling to contemplate the amount of suffering that the Lord has to bear to pay the debt for the sins of the billions of people that have lived and will yet live. He has to endure such terrible agony, beyond what any of us could survive.

He endures this torture in the Garden of Gethsemane for three or four hours, and then is met by a torch-light procession of soldiers and Jewish leaders that makes its way through the night led by

Judas Iscariot, one of the twelve apostles. He has been a close friend to Jesus but is now about to betray him.

It is amazing to me that the Savior, who has just suffered so severely for us, is now led away like a common criminal. That evening is to be spent in one of the most evil mockeries of a trial ever to take place. Jesus is found guilty of blasphemy, the most serious crime in their law, and is sentenced to death.

Next, he is interrogated by Pilate, beaten, has a crown of thorns jammed onto his head, and is spit upon and mocked by the soldiers as blood runs down his face.

The Savior is then led away to be crucified on Calvary. Nails are driven through his hands, wrists, and feet, and he is lifted up on the cross. He is placed on the cross at about nine o'clock in the morning, and finally, at about three in the afternoon, it is clear that our magnificent Savior finishes all that His Father sent him to earth to do and that his sacrifice is now complete and acceptable to the Father. Then we hear him utter, *"It is finished."* [6.3]

He voluntarily gives up His life: *"Father, into thy hands I commend my spirit, and having said thus, he gave up the ghost."*[6.4]

The peace and comfort of a merciful death finally frees Jesus Christ from the pains, tortures, and sorrows of the most horrible twenty-four-hour period ever endured. But it is also the most important display of courage, love, and unselfish service that has ever taken place!

Jesus Christ, Our Savior, Overcame Death

Later on Friday, the day the Savior was crucified, his body is placed in a tomb where it remains until Sunday morning. Then Mary Magdalene comes to the Garden Tomb and finds that it is empty.

We can read the tender account in John: *"But Mary stood without the sepulchre weeping: and as she wept, she stooped down, and looked into the sepulchre, And seeth two angels in white sitting, the one at the head, and the other at the feet, where the body of Jesus had lain. And they say unto her, Woman, why weepest thou? She saith unto them, Because they have taken away my Lord, and I know not where they have laid him. And when she had thus said, she turned herself back, and saw Jesus standing, and knew not that it was Jesus. Jesus saith unto her, Woman, why weepest thou? Whom seekest thou? She supposing him to be the gardener, saith unto him, Sir, if thou have borne him hence, tell me where thou hast laid him, and I will take him away. Jesus saith unto her, Mary. She turned herself, and saith unto him, Rabboni; which is to say Master."*[6.5]

After Jesus Christ appears to Mary, he also shows himself to a significant number of the other faithful followers, demonstrating that he has indeed overcome death, and in doing so opens the way for all of us to do the same.

The Savior has given to all the promise that we will be resurrected after we die and thus live again forever. On that glorious day after the Savior comes forth from his tomb, the scriptures record, "*And the graves were opened; and many bodies of the saints which slept arose. And came out of the graves after his resurrection, and went into the holy city, and appeared unto many.*"[6.6]

I am so grateful that this gift of immortality is given to all people, no matter how good or bad a life each of us may have lived. Paul puts it succinctly, "*For as in Adam all die, even so in Christ shall **all be made alive**.*"[6.7]

I believe that the most glorious news ever heard is "HE IS RISEN!" He has overcome death, hell, and the grave. He is the first to ever die and come back as a resurrected being who will never die again. This is the good news of the gospel of Jesus Christ: Our Savior has made it possible for us to live again after we die! I am so thankful that for the first time since the world began, humanity could have more than just a hope that there is life after death.

I do not think that the sacrifice Jesus made consisted of the Savior being murdered in spite of anything he could do to stop it. He had the power to keep his crucifixion from happening, but he allowed himself to be taken anyway. His offering had to be given freely. As the Savior said, "*No man taketh it from me, but I lay it down of myself, I have power to lay it down, and I have power to take it again.*"[6.8]

I believe the Savior did his part; now it is up to us to make sure that his magnificent gift helps us to the full extent that he intended. We must do everything we can to live righteously and to follow in the footsteps of the Savior. If we do this, he will make up for any of our deficits or shortcomings and will save us. It is by the grace of Jesus Christ that we are saved after all we can do.

Those who will not follow the Savior will be required to pay the price for their own sins and will disqualify themselves from ever being able to dwell with God again. It is equivalent to having the Savior enter the burning building to save someone, badly burning himself in the attempt, only to have them refuse to be rescued. They stubbornly stay in the burning building and needlessly endure the tortures of the flame and death. It is the ultimate misuse of their freedom of choice.

What Does the Savior's Sacrifice Mean for Us?

I believe that the Savior's sacrifice means that all of the hardships, pains, illnesses, disappointments, and injustices we suffer in this life will be more than made up for by the suffering of the Savior. He has made it possible for all of us to live again and to be forgiven of our mistakes. Through his suffering, he understands our sorrows and can therefore comfort us during our darkest and most difficult moments.

I think it is supremely important that we allow the Savior's great sacrifice to have a place in our lives. We do this by offering our Father in Heaven the only thing that is really ours to give, and that is our will— the will to follow Him and do as He asks, realizing that what He wants for us is better than what we sometimes want for ourselves.

We must be willing to follow the example of the Savior in the Garden of Gethsemane when he prayed to know if there was any way he could avoid the terrible tortures associated with his sacrifice. He finished the words of his prayer in a manner that reflected how he lived his life: *"Father, if thou be willing, remove this cup from me; nevertheless not my will, but thine, be done."*[6.9]

Once we learn to love Heavenly Father and Jesus Christ with all our hearts, we will learn to trust them and believe in all that they say. The Savior tells us in the fourteenth chapter of John, *"If ye love me, keep my commandments."*[6.10]

We must be willing to live the commandments he has given us: ask for forgiveness when we make mistakes, follow in the footsteps of the Savior, be baptized, serve others, and do all else that he asks of us.

When Saul, the anti-Christian who later became a faithful follower of Jesus Christ, was on his way to Damascus to persecute the Christians, he saw a light from heaven and heard a voice speaking to him. He responded with a simple yet powerful question that changed his life, *"Lord, what wilt thou have me to do?"*[6.11] I believe that if we ask this same question, it will also change our lives.

Our Pains, Sorrows, and Injustices Will Be More Than Compensated by the Savior

Our loving and wise Father knows of the difficulties, despair, and disappointments we suffer in this life, and He will not allow them to frustrate His plan to bless our lives. Jesus Christ also suffered loneliness, loss, rejection, and abuse, and thus can empathize with all of us who are imperfect. As Matthew explained, *"[He]. . .took our infirmities, and bare our sickness."*[6.12] Will any of us ever be able to say to the Savior, "You just do not understand what I had to go through, or the pain or anguish of soul that I had to endure"?

When we are able to look back on this life, we will see that every disappointment, injustice, or unfairness in our life will be more than made up for by what the Savior suffered for each of us and we will better understand why it was necessary to come to earth. We will feel that any temporary burdens or inconveniences we had to experience will have been more than repaid by the eternal inheritance of our kind and generous Father in Heaven.

What our Savior experienced during the last day he spent in mortality is the greatest event that has ever taken place in the history of the world.

Never has anything been done that has helped so many people in such a profound way. And so ends the most beautiful story of sacrifice, courage, and love known to man, a story filled with *"good tidings of great joy."*[6.13]

Because Jesus Christ lived a perfect life, He qualified to be the Savior of the world, the only one who could ransom us from physical and spiritual death.

He did all His Father asked of Him: lived a perfect life, suffered for our sins and afflictions, died, and was resurrected. In doing so, he gave us the promise of immortality and the hope of never-ending happiness in the kingdom of our Father.

Actions:

❖ Recognize that Jesus Christ was the perfect role model who taught us how to live and then demonstrated his teachings by the way he lived.

❖ Ponder the fact that you have made mistakes that make you ineligible to return to your heavenly home without the assistance of a mediator or savior.

❖ Express gratitude to your Father in Heaven for sending Jesus Christ to serve as your Savior and pay for your sins and mine by enduring the most awful agony ever experienced by man.

❖ Contemplate the fact that Jesus Christ died while on the cross and returned to life three days later as a resurrected being.

❖ Realize that the Jesus Christ's sacrifice is the most important event in your life because

  o He overcame death so that you will also overcome death and live forever.

  o He made it possible for you to be forgiven of your sins, which will enable you to return to live with your Heavenly Father *if* you do all that He has asked you to do.

❖ Understand that, because of the sacrifice of the Savior, all the hardships, disappointments, illnesses, pains, and injustices you suffered in this life will be more than made up to you.

Chapter Seven

What Happens When I Die?

———••———

I believe the subject of death should be of interest to all of us, as we will one day have to embrace it. However, there seems to be no subject that is avoided, shunned, or circumvented more than the topic of death. Perhaps some people are afraid to think about it. Others believe that death is the end of our existence, and since there is nothing we can do about it, why bother worrying about it?

A couple of years ago, I had the opportunity of seeing what happens when a person passes through the threshold of life. I went to the hospital to visit Al, a friend who had been in intensive care for nineteen days.

He asked if I would read to him. I picked up one of his books and began to read. Suddenly he stopped me and said, "I am ready to go. I do not want to live anymore. I want to die." This was the first time I had ever seen Al give up the will to live. He asked to be "unplugged" from the machines that had been keeping him alive.

I asked him if he would wait one more night, hoping that a night's sleep might change his mind. He agreed, and I arranged to come back to the hospital again the next morning. When I arrived the next day with two of his friends, he told us he still was of the same mind and wanted to die. The doctors said that since he had no family in the country and was of sound mind, they would do as he requested and unplug him from the medical equipment.

Then I saw one of the most amazing things I have ever seen in my life. In less than two minutes from the time the machines were disconnected, Al's color completely changed and he died. It was as if the light that was in him went out.

Al's passing caused me to think once again about that question that I assume all of us have pondered: "What happens when we die?" Some people believe that, after our life on the earth is over, there is nothing more. The famed scientist Marie Curie recorded such feelings in her journal after returning from burying her husband, who had died in an accident in Paris. She wrote, *"They filled the grave and put sheaves of flowers on it. Everything is over. Pierre is sleeping his last sleep beneath the earth. It is the end of everything, everything, everything."*

I do not believe as Madame Curie did. What a sad and hopeless existence this life would be if this is all there was. However, if we could get but a glimpse of what happens to us in the next stage of our existence, when our eyes close on mortality and open on eternity, we would know that death is nothing to fear. What could be more natural than a son or daughter returning home to their Father?

This vital truth became clear to me one evening as I was sitting with my seven-year-old daughter watching a movie. When the life of the hero seemed to hang in the balance and it looked like he might die, she looked up at me and said, "Daddy, it's all right if you die, if you go back to heaven to live with Heavenly Father." I was touched by her wisdom and faith.

Perhaps when we talk about people being dead, it is a misrepresentation. When we pass from mortality we are still alive, and in many respects much more so than before. We have departed from a life of sorrow, grief, disappointment, misery, pain, and anguish and have graduated into the next stage of our existence. When we pass through the doorway of death and enter the exciting next phase of our eternal development, our kind and loving Heavenly Father will open additional panoramas to our view. Yes, the Creator of the Universe is also in charge of what happens next to His children and is mindful of our every need.

What is Death?

I believe that death is the separation of our spirit body from our physical body. When we die, our physical body decays and returns to the elements of the earth. Our spirit body, which was placed inside of our physical body to give it life at the time of our birth, continues to exist, allowing us to think, decide, and take action. Without it, there would be no life in us. As the words of the Psalmist state, *"thou takest away their breath, they die, and return to their dust."*[7.1]

Someone has compared the process of dying to taking your hand out of a glove. Your hand represents your spirit body and the glove represents your physical body. When your hand is in the glove, you can move it around and there is life and vitality in the glove. But when your hand is withdrawn from the glove, it becomes limp and immobile. If the hand were placed back into the glove, it would again move and have life. If the spirit came back into the body, it would have life again.

This is exactly what happened when Jesus Christ restored life to the twelve-year-old daughter of a man named Jairus, the ruler of the synagogue.

When Jairus came to the Savior, he fell down at his feet and begged him to heal his daughter. *"While he yet spake, there cometh one from the ruler of the synagogue's house, saying to him Thy daughter is dead; trouble not the Master. But when Jesus heard it, he answered him saying, Fear not: believe only, and she shall be made whole. And he*

came into the house, he suffered no man to go in, save Peter,
and James and John, and the father and the mother of the
maiden. And all wept, and bewailed her; but he said, Weep
not; she is not dead, but sleepeth. And they laughed him to
scorn, knowing that she was dead. And he put them all out,
and took her by the hand, and called, saying, Maid, arise.
*And **her spirit came again,** and she arose straightway:*
and he commanded to give her meat."[7.2]

Passing Through the Threshold of Life

Many of us have seen what happens when a person
dies: Their physical body becomes cold and lifeless
and no longer has their spirit inside of it. Our body
cannot live without the spirit. As the Apostle James
said, ". . . *The body without the spirit is dead. . ."*[7.3]

Since our Father placed us on earth to learn and to
grow, we do not suddenly cease to exist after our
physical body dies. Rather, I think we will be even
more vibrant and alive in the next stage of our
existence than we ever were in mortality. I also believe
we will have an increased understanding of why we
were placed on the earth. I remember a wonderful
lady by the name of Lenore telling me how she gained
an increased understanding of life as she watched her
friend, Leslie, pass through the doorway of life.

She said, "Leslie was determined to not let any
disease get the better of her. She made an appointment
in San Francisco to see a specialist who had an
excellent reputation, feeling certain he would be able
to help her. However, I'll never forget seeing her the

next day. Her fighting spirit was gone and she was bitterly angry. The news had not been good. The doctor not only diagnosed the illness as terminal but he also turned her over to a hospice care unit. Her hope was smashed to pieces. She projected her anger on her deceased husband for leaving her alone to deal with it. With this, the dying process had begun."

"It was difficult to see her deteriorate so rapidly. Her anger seemed to be poisoning her and kept her from finding peace and comfort. One day we had a discussion about life, the purpose of our trials, and the fact that our Father in Heaven does not remove all the burdens in life but instead gives us strength to deal with them if we but ask. I suggested to her that we can't always control situations in life, but we can choose our response or attitude concerning them."

"The next day Leslie seemed peaceful. She thanked me for helping her to see her trials differently. The anger was gone, and I was able to talk about the Savior and the power of his sacrifice in our behalf, how he understands our situation, and how he can comfort us. I promised that she would come to know him, and I prayed she would feel the Savior's love and would allow him to comfort her."

"She was in a coma the next day when I walked in. I sat down next to her bed, and an hour later she opened her eyes. I held her in my arms and comforted her.   I stroked her head and tried to make her comfortable. Time was fleeing. She asked, '*Am I coming or going?*' I told her she was *coming...* to a beautiful place where she would be surrounded by love. She smiled and opened her eyes and whispered over and over to me, *'He paid the price.'* My prayer was answered. She had come to feel the Savior's love for herself."

"She was going fast now. I cradled her one last time in my arms and then kissed her tenderly on her forehead, cheeks, and hands. Having never witnessed death before, I found it profound. Not much was said, but there was a certain reverence that felt very sacred."

"Leslie was frightened in the beginning, but as death reached out and drew her closer, she was able to let go and to be calm. In the end, Leslie's illness didn't beat her; it helped her to be more humble and to feel closer to the Savior."

Where Do We Go After We Die?

What happens once we die and our spirit body, which lived with Heavenly Father before we came to earth, leaves our physical body? I found help in understanding the answer to this question in Ecclesiastes, a book in the Old Testament that looks at the transitory and fleeting nature of earth life.

When referring to death, it states: *"Then shall the dust [physical body] return to the earth as it was: and the spirit shall return unto God who gave it."*[7.4]

As the Bible tells us, when we die our body is left here on earth to return to the dust from which it came, and our spirit returns to God.

All People Will Have the Chance To Hear the Words of Jesus Christ

Before our spirit returns to God, there appears to be a stop along the way. The apostle Peter explains the reason: *"For Christ also hath once suffered for sins, the just for the unjust, that he might bring us to God. . . .By which also he went and preached unto the spirits in prison."*[7.5]

Peter tells us that Jesus went to preach to the spirits of those who had died. Then he says, *"For this cause was the gospel preached also to them that are dead, that they might be judged according to men in the flesh,. . . "*[7.6]

Peter states that the gospel is preached to the dead in order that they might be judged. Therefore, I assume that we are not judged until after we go to the world of the spirits, or the spirit world.

This concept makes sense to me because it gives everyone the chance to hear the teachings of Jesus Christ. If we do not hear them before we die, then we can hear them in the spirit world so that all of us will have the opportunity to accept or reject his teachings before we are judged.

I remember hearing a man give a talk on the subject of what happens after we die. This speaker indicated that he was once approached by a minister who said that he believed that no one can be saved who does not accept Jesus Christ before they die.

The speaker said that he was a little surprised at the minister's attitude and asked him 'what will happen to the two billion people living on the earth at this time who will die without even hearing the name of Jesus Christ?' The minister shocked him with his cavalier and callous response when he said with the wave of his hand, "It is just too bad about them."

I firmly believe that such thinking reflects a lack of understanding of the nature of our Heavenly Father. I know that our perfect, just, merciful, and loving Father in Heaven would not be unfair to any of His children, for to do so would be an imperfection.

Would it be fair for a person to be held back, damned, or judged for not following the teachings of Jesus Christ if they never had the chance to learn of his teachings? What opportunity would a person have to follow in the footsteps of Jesus Christ if they lived in a primitive village in the Amazon jungle, or a remote community in the heart of Africa, or in a nation that forbids the teaching of Christianity?

What about the people who are mentally incapable of understanding Christ's teachings, or those who die as babies? Realistically, they would have little or no chance of being able to embrace the life-saving truths taught by the Savior.

I would ask, "How does a just and fair God reconcile such inequality of opportunity?" What will become of the people through the centuries who have lived and died upon this earth without having had the opportunity of hearing the teachings of Jesus Christ?

Unlike the minister mentioned above, who with the wave of his hand was willing to write off two billion of God's children, I believe that Heavenly Father has provided the opportunity for each of His children to hear the teachings of the Savior.

If we do not hear the vital truths our Father wants us to hear while we are on earth, I believe we will have the chance to hear them after we die. The apostle John records these words from the Savior: *"The hour is coming, and now is, when the dead shall hear the voice of the Son of God: and they that hear shall live."*[7.7]

Going to the World of Spirits

I think that once we die and go to the world of spirits, our friends and loved ones who went before us will be there to embrace us. I imagine it will be a precious time of re-acquaintance, where relationships will be renewed and friendships remembered.

How great will be the reunion we will have with those we knew so well here on earth. I do not believe that the loving relationships we form in this life will be forgotten after we die. Rather, I believe that each friend or loved one that precedes us in death serves as a magnet to make entering the next stage of our existence more inviting for us when our turn comes.

No More Physical Pain, but the Same Attitude and Disposition

I assume that while we are in the spirit world, awaiting the day of judgment and resurrection, we will be able to lay aside many of the issues that dominated our time and attention in mortality. Any illness, physical pain, disease, or other infirmities that were associated with our physical body will be gone.

However, I believe we will still have the same personality we possessed in this life. If we were sweet, loving, and caring while on earth, we will have those same characteristics when we are dead. If we were selfish, uncaring, and unbelieving here in mortality, we will be the same in the next stage of our existence.

After all, the reason we came to earth is to develop our character and personality. We accomplish this over a lifetime through the choices we make and the things we do; therefore, I believe it is logical that the character we have developed in this life is the one that will continue with us after we die.

Entering Paradise or Prison

If we have lived an honorable life, followed the commandments that our Father in Heaven has given us, and accepted Jesus Christ, we will be happy in the next life, where we will find ourselves in a condition referred to as *paradise*. I think paradise in the spirit world is a condition of peace and happiness, where we will not be focused on the cares, troubles, and hardships of the world. There we will find great joy while we wait for the rest of God's children to have the chance to hear the words of the Savior.

Those who never heard or who rejected the message of the Savior in this life will be in what the apostle Peter referred to as *prison*, where Jesus Christ went to preach. Once in the spirit prison, those who have never heard the life-giving words of the Savior may readily accept them and will then be able to join those in paradise. But those who have hardened their hearts and rejected the Savior's sacrifice for them are destined to remain in a state of torment until they have suffered for their own sins.

I doubt that those in spirit prison are permitted to mingle freely with those in paradise. In the parable the Lord teaches about the rich man and Lazarus, we learn more about the separation of the two divisions in the spirit world. *"There was a certain rich man, which was clothed in purple and fine linen, and fared sumptuously every day: And there was a certain beggar named Lazarus, which was laid at his gate, full of sores. And it came to pass, that the beggar died, and was carried by the angels into Abraham's bosom; the rich man also died, and was buried; And in hell he lift up his eyes, being in torments, and seeth Abraham afar off, and Lazarus in his bosom. And he cried and said, Father Abraham, have mercy on me, and send Lazarus, that he may dip the tip of his finger in water, and cool my tongue; for I am tormented in this flame. But Abraham said, Son, remember that thou in thy lifetime receivedst thy good things, and likewise Lazarus evil things:*

but now he is comforted, and thou art tormented. And besides all this, between us and you there is a great gulf fixed: so that they which would pass from hence to you cannot; neither can they pass to us, that would come from thence. "[7,8]

However, as Peter told us, the gulf between paradise and prison was bridged by Jesus Christ when he was in the spirit world, after he died on the cross. I think it is very likely that in the spirit world, as on earth, those who have lived honorable lives and accepted the gospel of Jesus Christ will be given the opportunity to take his message to those in spirit prison.

They will teach them that they can be freed from the shackles of ignorance and sin by learning of Jesus Christ and keeping his commandments. I suppose they will explain that the Lord's suffering and sacrifice have already paid the price for their sins. If they will repent and live the commandments of God, there is no reason that they must remain in spirit prison and pay the debt that our Savior has already paid for them.

I think that it is logical that our just and merciful Father will allow those in spirit prison who have repented and made a commitment to live the gospel of Jesus Christ to leave their spirit prison and join those who are in spirit paradise. I believe that those who move from spirit prison to paradise will be able to await the day of resurrection and judgment with the hope of gaining immortality and living in the realms of heaven forever with the righteous.

Those who refuse to accept his message will remain in spirit prison until the final judgment day. Until that day they will have to endure the agony, anguish, and torment that the Savior already experienced for them when he suffered in the Garden of Gethsemane and on the cross.

The time we spend in the spirit world, like our time on earth, is given to us so we can continue to progress and grow. Our stay in the spirit world is a temporary one and will end when we are resurrected and assigned to a kingdom of glory according to how we lived our lives.

Our ultimate destination when we leave the spirit world and are resurrected will be greater than we can imagine. It is a never-ending existence that is free from physical pain, sickness, loneliness, and worry. And if we have lived the commandments that our Father has given us, we will be able to return to live with Him and have a joyous existence beyond our comprehension.

Actions:

❖ Realize that your kind and loving Heavenly Father sent you to earth to learn and to grow, and when your time on earth is over, you will die and begin the next stage of your existence.

❖ Understand that when death takes place,

   o Your physical body of flesh and bone is separated from your spirit body.

o   Your physical body that is made up of the elements returns to the earth.

o   Your spirit body that existed before you came to earth moves on to begin the next stage of progression.

o   Your spirit will first go to the world of spirits where you will have the chance to be reacquainted with many of your friends and loved ones who preceded you in death.

o   Your spirit body will no longer be subject to the pains, illnesses, or other infirmities that were associated with the physical body.

o   Your same character and personality that you possessed on earth will continue with you in the next stage of your life.

o   You will be assigned to paradise or prison in the spirit world, depending upon how you lived your life while on earth.

o   You will be taught about the teachings of Jesus Christ if you have not already accepted them.

❖   Realize that death is nothing to fear, as what could be more natural than a son or daughter returning home to their Father?

Chapter Eight

What is the Resurrection and Judgment?

——•——

I believe there is a great deal to look forward to after death. We will all be resurrected and someday have the opportunity to receive a wonderful inheritance from our Heavenly Father. However, before we focus on inheriting a kingdom of glory, let's look at what happens when we are resurrected and judged according to the accounting of how we have lived our life.

What Is Resurrection?

We learn from reading the Bible that resurrection is the reuniting of the physical body and the spirit, which were separated at death. When we are resurrected, our body and our spirit are joined together and become immortal, never to be separated again. The best example we have of a person being resurrected is the account of the Savior.

After Jesus Christ was crucified and died on that Friday afternoon nearly 2,000 years ago, he was put into a tomb and a stone was placed to seal the grave. The following Sunday two angels were sent to the tomb, and they rolled away the stone. Later that morning, Mary Magdalene came to the tomb, saw that it was empty, and inquired concerning the whereabouts of Jesus' body. Then one of the angelic messengers conveyed those most glorious words, *"He is not here, for HE IS RISEN.*"[8.1]

For the first time in the history of the world, someone who had died came forth from the grave as a resurrected being, never to die again, and in so doing he opened the way for all of us to be able to do the same. I am so thankful that the time we spend on this earth is not all there is to our existence.

This knowledge gives me hope and encouragement and motivates me to do my best while I am here on earth.

What Will Our Resurrected Body Be Like?

On the day the Savior was resurrected, the apostles were meeting together when they were visited by the risen Lord. *"And as they thus spake, Jesus himself stood in the midst of them, and saith unto them, Peace be unto you. But they were terrified and affrighted, and supposed that they had seen a spirit. And he said unto them, Why are ye troubled? And why do thoughts arise in your hearts? Behold my hands and my feet, that it is I myself: handle me, and see; for a spirit hath not flesh and bones, as ye see me have. And when he had thus spoken, he shewed them his hands and his feet.*"[8.2]

And while the resurrected Christ was meeting with his apostles he asked them, "*Have ye here any meat? And they gave him a piece of a broiled fish, and of an honeycomb. And he took it, and did eat before them.*"[8.3]

It is clear from this account that our resurrected bodies will be able to eat and digest food. I believe that once we have been resurrected, we will have tangible bodies of flesh and bone, as did the Savior. These bodies will look much like those we possessed while on earth, but they will not be subject to illness, aging, or death.

All Will Be Resurrected?

As the apostle Paul said, "*But now is Christ risen from the dead, and become the firstfruits of them that slept. For since by man came death, by man came also the resurrection of the dead. For as in Adam all die, even so in Christ shall all be made alive.*"[8.4]

The fall of Adam brought about death, and the resurrection of Christ overcame physical death and made it possible for *all* who live on the earth to be resurrected.

Apparently there are no prerequisites to being resurrected other than to have lived on the earth.

Resurrection is something that each and every one of us can look forward to with anticipation.

We have all been promised this wonderful gift, no matter how good or bad our lives were while we were on the earth. Resurrection is a free gift to all of us.

Isaiah's prophecy about the death and resurrection of the Savior says, "*He will swallow up death in victory;*"[8.5] and Paul's elaboration on this prophecy, "*O death, where is thy sting? O grave, where is thy victory,*"[8.6] was fulfilled with Christ's resurrection. I believe that each of us will receive a resurrected body that will never be subject to pain, disease, aging or death. However, I think that the quality of our future existence will vary dramatically depending on our obedience to God's commandments.

When Will We Be Resurrected?

After the Savior opened the passageway for all to be able to come forth from the grave, many of the dead were resurrected. Matthew records, "*And the graves were opened; and many bodies of the saints which slept arose. And came out of the graves after his resurrection, and went into the holy city, and appeared unto many.*"[8.7]

The faithful followers of Christ who lived and died prior to the death of the Savior were resurrected just after he was resurrected.

The time of the resurrection for all who have lived and died since the Savior lived on the earth will be when Jesus Christ comes again. When the Savior returns to the earth, the resurrection will continue in an orderly way. As the apostle Paul says, *"But every man in his own order: Christ the firstfruits; afterward they that are Christ's at his coming . . . For he must reign, till he hath put all enemies under his feet. The last enemy that shall be destroyed is death."*[8.8]

Then Paul goes on to explain that when Christ comes back to the earth, He will bring those who will be resurrected to join Him and stay with Him forever. He says, *"For if we believe that Jesus died and rose again, even so them also which sleep in Jesus will God bring with him. For the Lord himself shall descend from heaven with a shout with the voice of the archangel, and with the trump of God; and the dead in Christ shall rise first. Then we which are alive and remain shall be caught up together with them in the clouds, to meet the Lord in the air: and so shall we ever be with the Lord."*[8.9]

I think it is important to realize that the more righteous we are, the sooner we will be resurrected. The first to come forth will be those who were valiant in living the truth that they were given and in testifying of the divinity of Jesus Christ as the Son of God. Those who were generally good people on earth but who were not righteous enough to come forth when the Savior returns will remain in the spirit world until all those who were valiant have had a chance to come forth.

And those who remain hardened and rebellious will not come forth from the spirit world until the second resurrection. John points this out in Revelation:

"I saw the souls of them that ... lived and reigned with Christ a thousand years. But the rest of the dead lived not again until the thousand years were finished."[8.10] This resurrection will take place after the millennium, or the thousand-year period when Christ will reign upon the earth, has ended.

The Old Testament prophet Daniel explains that once we are resurrected the reward that awaits us will vary dramatically: *"And many of them that sleep in the dust of the earth shall awake, some to everlasting life, and some to shame and everlasting contempt."*[8.11] John reaffirms this by quoting the Savior: *"Marvel not at this: for the hour is coming, in the which all that are in the graves shall hear his voice, and shall come forth; they that have done good, unto the resurrection of life; and they that have done evil, unto the resurrection of damnation."*[8.12]

I believe that God is kind and loving, but I also believe that he is just and fair and will reward us according to the kind of life we chose to live. If we do what he asks us to do, we will have a great deal to look forward to. But if we refuse to do what he asks, we will be very sorry.

A Preliminary Judgment

Before the final judgment takes place, I believe there will be a preliminary judgment that takes place right after we die, when we will be temporarily assigned to go to either spirit paradise or spirit prison, the two divisions in the spirit world. The spirit world is the staging area where we will go to await the day of resurrection and judgment.

Those who have accepted the Father and His Son and have lived their commandments are assigned to spirit paradise. Those who have either rejected these teachings or have never had the opportunity to hear about them are assigned to spirit prison. There, a just and fair God provides the chance, for all who did not have that opportunity during their lifetime to learn about the Savior.

What Will Judgment Be Like?

After we leave the spirit world and are resurrected, we will be judged, an event that we have been preparing for our entire life, whether we realize it or not.

"Hey, wait a minute," you may ask, "why will we be judged? If our Heavenly Father loves us so much, why do we have to go through the ordeal of being judged? After all, doesn't Heavenly Father want us all to return to live with Him?" The answer is yes, our Father in Heaven loves us and yes, He would like all of us to return to live with Him."

However, we must consider that our ultimate destiny is not completely up to our Father in Heaven, for He has given us the freedom to choose what our future will be like. We choose the things we will do in life, and the consequences of our actions come as a natural result of our choices.

It is also important to realize that we would not feel comfortable living in a heavenly paradise with people who are virtuous, lovely, and pure if we did not possess the same characteristics they did. We would feel self-conscious and out of place.

Another factor that is vital to consider is the fact that since our Heavenly Father is a just God, He must hold us accountable for how we lived the commandments we were given. If it did not matter whether or not we lived His commandments, why would anyone bother to obey Him? If there were not a day of reckoning when God held us accountable, then He would not be a perfect, truthful, or just God.

During the day of judgment, I imagine we will think back on all the things we wish we had done or not done. This test, the only one that really matters, is our final accounting of what we did with the time, resources, and opportunities we were given on earth.

A few months ago, I read an article in a popular magazine about an interview with a very well known celebrity. One of the questions the reporter asked him was regarding his faith. The celebrity responded that he believed that after death there would be a judgment day, at which time God will judge how we lived our life. If our bad deeds outweigh the good, we go to hell, but if our good deeds outweigh the bad, we go to heaven. He said that this belief influences how he treats people because he feels his actions are being recorded and that one day he will have to give a final accounting of his life.

Perhaps these sentiments, which helped this man live a good life, are similar to the beliefs of many. However, I do not think this is how a just God operates. Yes, our actions are being recorded; but our Father does not place all our good deeds on one side of the balance and all our sins on the other side, sending us to heaven if there is more good and to hell if there is more bad.

We Will Be Judged by the Content of Our Character

The Lord looks at more than just our actions. He also takes into account our words and thoughts and the intents of our hearts. We will be judged on the content of our character, a character that has been developed over a lifetime.

As Malachi explains, God will also hold us accountable for how we treated those who were most vulnerable: *"And I will come near to you to judgment; and I will be a swift witness against the sorcerers, and against the adulterers, and against false swearers, and against those that oppress the hireling in his wages, the widow, the fatherless, and that turn aside the stranger from his right, and fear not me. . . ."*[8.13]

The Saddest Words in Time or Eternity

On the day of judgment, some people will lament and suffer because they will realize the eternal consequences of their choices. It is then that they will realize the heavy price they must pay for having decided to do things *"my way"* instead of listening to the promptings of their conscience and following the Savior. The consequences are severe:

They will have to suffer the mental and emotional distress of knowing what might have been. I think that for the rest of eternity they will often contemplate the alternate course they might have pursued and voice those most disheartening words, *"If only,"* or as John Greenleaf Whitter put it,

"Of all sad words of tongue or pen, The saddest are these: 'It might have been!'" (Maud Miller, The Complete Poetical Works of Whitter, 1892 p.48).

Our Father in Heaven Will Hold Us Accountable

The process of judgment is very thorough. In Ecclesiastes we read, *"Fear God, and keep his commandments: for this is the whole duty of man. For God shall bring every work into judgment, with every secret thing, whether it be good, or whether it be evil."*[8.14] In Matthew, the Lord says, *"But I say unto you, That every idle word that men shall speak, they shall give account thereof in the day of judgment."*[8.15] I think it is clear that our Father in Heaven will hold us accountable for all of our thoughts, feelings, words and actions.

The Bible tells us that an account of our life is not only being recorded, but on the day of judgment it will reveal to everyone the kind of person we really are. John explains: "*And I saw the dead, small and great stand before God; and the books were opened: and another book was opened which is the book of life: and the dead were judged out of those things which were written in the books, according to their works.*"[8.16]

It may surprise us to see that the many acts of kindness, love, and charity that we have performed will also be brought to light. I believe we will see played out before us the positive things we have done, including lifting the burdens of others, brightening the day of those who were lonely, helping one in need, and standing up for people who were not accepted. And then the Savior's words recorded in the twenty-fifth chapter of Matthew will take on a special meaning to us: "*Verily I say unto you, inasmuch as ye have done it unto one of the least of these my brethren, ye have done it unto me.*"[8.17]

There is No Limit to the Number Who Can Return to Live with Our Father in Heaven

Because He loves us, our Father wants every one of us as His children to return to live with Him. Therefore, it seems logical that the slots available in heaven are not limited. Father does not operate on a quota system, nor does He grade on a curve that would only allow the top 10% of us to be able to return to our heavenly home.

If every one of us were to follow in the Savior's footsteps, we would all return to be with our

Heavenly Father for the rest of eternity. We are all invited!

We Can Be Rescued

As we stand to be judged, I think we will long for someone to defend us and help us during this critical time. Maybe we will want someone like the high-priced and celebrated attorneys here on earth, who are able to obtain the desired verdict regardless of their client's guilt or innocence.

I believe that in the royal courts above, things will be different. There, justice will not give way to clever argument or showmanship, and there will be only one who is qualified to represent us: our Savior, Jesus Christ.

By the time we are standing to be judged, we will have already decided whether the Savior will represent us or whether we will represent ourselves. If we have chosen to follow in his footsteps and live the commandments he has given us, he will be there to plead our case. If we have chosen to walk our own path in life, we will discover the meaning of real loneliness and despair.

Some time ago, I heard the following story that I thought was a good analogy of how the Savior's advocacy will work for us when we are in front of the judgment bar of God.

During the Civil War, a nineteen-year-old Union Army soldier fell asleep while on guard duty, allowing the Confederate troops to break through their lines and kill many Union soldiers. Later this young soldier was court-marshaled and sentenced to die. A death warrant was prepared and sent to President Abraham Lincoln for signature.

The mother of the condemned soldier sought an audience with President Lincoln. When she was finally able to meet with the president, she said, "My son knows that what he did cost many people their lives and he believes that he deserves to die. I am not arguing the justice of his sentence, either; but when the war started I had a husband and 6 sons, and all have died in the war except him, my last son, who is now sentenced to die. Will you please spare him as he is all I have left?" President Lincoln said, "For your sake, because you have already given so much, I will spare him."

We Cannot Save Ourselves

It is very important to realize that no matter how good a life we live, and how many good deeds we perform in our life, we cannot save ourselves. We as imperfect beings cannot pay the price for our own sins and earn our way into heaven. It is impossible to overcome death and be resurrected to a kingdom of glory without Jesus Christ's sacrifice. There is only one person who can save us, and that is our Savior, Jesus Christ.

I can just imagine how we will feel as we stand in front of the judgment bar with a clear recollection of the things we have done wrong. Our appreciation and gratitude for Jesus Christ will be magnified beyond our understanding as we realize that He has *made it possible* for each unworthy act, thought, and word to be wiped away, never to be remembered again.

The Savior did this through his suffering. He fulfilled the demands of justice for each and every one of us. *If* we have accepted Jesus Christ and tried to live his commandments, he will be able to say to our Father, "I know he has made many mistakes, but he has repented for the things he has done wrong and he did the best he could to live a good life and to keep the commandments we gave him. Since I have suffered for his sins, will you spare him?"

Our Father will say to the Savior, "Yes, for your sake I will spare him." Then the errors of our life can be placed forever behind us, and we will no longer be held accountable for them. We will then qualify to return to our heavenly home. No one else but Jesus Christ can be our advocate and save us. Sadly, those who do not follow the Savior will be required to suffer for their own sins and will disqualify themselves from ever being able to return to dwell with God again.

Kingdoms Of Glory

It is not unusual to read novels and other literary works that suggest that the ultimate destiny of man will be a utopian paradise or a torturous hell. But that is like saying that all of God's children can receive only one of two grades, an A or an F, in spite of the vast variation in the way people have lived their lives. I believe that the plan of our all-wise Heavenly Father is much more comprehensive and fair than this simple concept.

The Savior explained to his apostles, "*In my Father's house are* **many** *mansions: if it were not so, I would have told you. I go to prepare a place for you.*"[8.18] I believe that once the day of judgment has arrived, our just, fair, and loving Father will reward each of us according to how we have lived. This by necessity means that there **must be many categories of rewards.**

If we have not lived a life that is suitable to be able to return to live with our Father in Heaven, then we will be given as an inheritance a kingdom of glory that will be dwelling place where we can be comfortable and prosper. I believe that our loving and merciful Father will give us all that he can, while still remaining fair and just.

However, if we have maximized our opportunities by following the Savior's teachings, our inheritance from our Heavenly Father will be a glorified, magnificent, resurrected body that is no longer subject to decay, aging, or death and an invitation to return to live in our heavenly home for eternity.

I believe that if we qualify to return to live with our Heavenly Father again, we will have been magnified and glorified to the point that we can dwell in His presence forever. The glory and joy of this existence will be beyond our current comprehension! It will be worth anything we must do to be able to inherit this glorious existence!

Actions:

❖ Ponder the fact that no matter how good a life you live, and how many good deeds you perform, you cannot save yourself; you need your Savior's help.

❖ Realize that Jesus Christ was the first person to ever come forth from the grave as a resurrected being, never to die again, and opened the way for you to do the same.

❖ Understand that when you are resurrected your spirit and body will be reunited and you will inherit an immortal body that will never again be subject to pain, illness, disease, aging, or death.

❖ Recognize that the resurrection that was made possible by the Savior, is a free gift which is given to you and **everyone** else who will live on the earth.

❖ Understand that you will be judged on the content of your character, which is developed during your lifetime by the things you do and by your thoughts and feelings.

❖ Live the commandments that the Savior has given you, and his sacrifice will pay for your sins and he will stand as your advocate on the day of judgment.

❖ Anticipate that you will receive as an inheritance, a kingdom of glory that will reflect how you have lived your life and followed the teachings of Jesus Christ.

❖ Express gratitude to your loving Father in Heaven for His beautiful plan of salvation, which provides the opportunity for you to be able to return to live with Him and share a never-ending, glorious life of peace and joy.

Summary

The Plan of Love, Life, and Happiness

———•·•———

I am in awe of the wisdom and beauty contained in the plan our Heavenly Father has put in place to bless His children. He who knows when a sparrow falls to the ground is mindful of each of us. With divine understanding, wisdom, mercy, and love, He will reward each of us with a future that is fitting for what we have prepared ourselves to receive while in this life.

Prior to coming to earth, we lived as either a son or a daughter of God. In this heavenly realm, we were born as spirit children to Heavenly Parents. We were carefully taught and guided, and we grew and developed.

Then the time came for us to leave our heavenly home so we could continue to progress. A beautiful planet was provided for us to live on, one filled with variety and all the things that we would need to be able to succeed.

Each of us is sent to earth to obtain a body of flesh and bone to clothe our immortal spirit and to be tested to see if we will do what our Father has asked us to do in order to return to our heavenly home.

We are here to learn to control our appetites, passions, and desires and to strive to develop an honorable character similar to that of our Father in Heaven.

When we are born to earthly parents, a veil is drawn across our minds so that we do not remember our prior existence in the heavenly realms. This requires us to learn to walk by faith. Our Father in Heaven has given us the special opportunity of being able to choose for ourselves how we will think, feel, and live while on earth.

Father has also given each of us a moral compass called our conscience. It prompts us to do right and warns us when we are tempted to do wrong. If we will follow its promptings, we will be led to the light and truth that Heavenly Father will give us. When we choose correctly, we are given more light and knowledge from our Father in Heaven. When our choices are unwise, our progress is slowed, hindered, or stopped.

We must also be aware of and resist the forces of evil, which are led by Satan, or the Devil. The forces of evil fight against all that is good and virtuous and strive to make all of us as miserable as they are by tempting us to rebel against everything our Father wants for us.

Heavenly Father has placed us on earth to learn, progress, and grow. Although He gives each of us the freedom to choose the life we will live, He does not give us the freedom to choose the consequences that come as a result of our choices. The thousands of decisions we make in this life determine what kind of person we become.

If we choose to give in to the temptations of he who seeks our destruction, we will reap heartache and sorrow. But if we serve and love God and our fellowmen, are guided by our conscience, and do the things Father has asked of us, we will not only fulfill our purpose for being on earth but we will also find great joy in this life and in the life to come. We will build a character that is filled with integrity and that will feel *comfortable* in the presence of divine purity, kindness, and love.

Heavenly Father knew we would all make mistakes that would render us ineligible to return to our heavenly home. Therefore, He selected Jesus Christ to be our Savior, master teacher, and role model and to pay the debt for all of the mistakes we will make during our lifetime.

If we will accept him as our Savior and live his commandments, he will carry the burden of our sins. We will not have to suffer for our mistakes if we live the teachings of Jesus Christ.

Jesus Christ has taught us the importance of praying to the Father and asking Him for help. Prayer is the ability to bring the power of heaven into our lives to help us. There is no challenge or trial we will face in this life that we cannot handle if we have the assistance of Heavenly Father. All things go better with prayer!

We will all experience hardships and challenges in this life that are very frustrating and discouraging and that try our patience. These experiences cause us to struggle, to work, and to grow as they test our resolve to succeed in life.

They also give us the opportunity to increase our wisdom and understanding and to prepare ourselves for the next stage of our existence. For how could we really appreciate a body that was free of pain and disease if we had never been ill?

How could we really appreciate a body that was immortal if we had never experienced death? Could we really appreciate eternal happiness if we had never known disappointment, despair, or discouragement?

To be truly happy, we need to have a positive attitude and actions and, most importantly, faith in Jesus Christ and the fact that he suffered so that we wouldn't have to. We develop faith in Christ by being humble and meek enough to do what our Father has asked us to do.

After our life on earth is finished and we die, our physical body returns to the earth and our spirit body goes to the spirit world. If we have lived the commandments that the Savior has given us and followed in his footsteps, we go to spirit paradise; if not, we go to spirit prison.

If we have not had a chance to hear the words of Jesus Christ, we will be given that opportunity in spirit prison. And if we believe the Savior's teachings and repent of our sins, we will be accepted into spirit paradise. We will remain in the spirit world only until it is time for each of us to receive our immortal body, through the resurrection.

When Jesus Christ was resurrected, he made it possible for all of us to be resurrected. Everyone will receive a resurrected body and will live forever. When we are resurrected, our spirit will once again be reunited with our physical body. Then our resurrected bodies will never again be subject to pain, illness, or death.

Once everyone has been resurrected, we will all stand before the judgment bar of God to give an accounting of how we have lived our lives. The Savior has made it possible for each unworthy act, thought, and word that has been a part of our life to be purged, never to be remembered again.

He will serve as our advocate to plead our case and to take upon himself the punishment for our mistakes. Once we have been cleansed by the Savior, we can qualify to return to our heavenly home.

In order to qualify for these eternal blessings, we must do everything we can to live righteously and to follow the Savior. If we do this, he will make up for any deficits or shortcomings we have.

Those who will not accept and follow the Savior will be required to pay the price for their own sins and will disqualify themselves from ever being able to return to dwell with God again.

Our Father in Heaven has prepared a variety of rewards for His children. Each of us will be assigned to a kingdom of glory that will be commensurate with how we have lived, and we will be placed in an environment where we will be most comfortable.

I know Heavenly Father loves us and is aware of our wants and needs. He will bless us if we will pray and ask for His help. I love Him with all my heart and am grateful that He is so kind, merciful, and forgiving.

I am also eternally grateful to our Savior who did so very much for us. He suffered terribly so we would not need to suffer. He also broke the bands of death and provided each of us the opportunity to live a never-ending life of unspeakable joy in the realms of heaven. I encourage you, too, to learn more about the purpose of our life here on earth. As you sincerely seek the truth, your life will be blessed.

Recap of Actions:

Chapter 1

Who Am I?

❖ Appreciate and be thankful for the beauty, order and intricacy of the world we live in.

❖ Contemplate the fact that you are created in the likeness and image of God.

❖ Remember that you are a child of God and are related to the Creator of the Universe who wants you to call Him Father.

❖ Understand that your Father in Heaven cares about you and wants to help you.

❖ Bring the power of heaven into your life each day by calling upon Heavenly Father in prayer.

❖ Remember you are never alone as long as you invite Heavenly Father into your life.

Chapter 2

Where Did I Come From?

❖ Ponder the fact that you lived in a heavenly home with your Father in Heaven before you were born.

❖   Understand that you were nurtured and tutored by your loving Heavenly Father until it was time for you to come to earth.

❖   Consider the reality that you were sent to earth to continue to learn, progress, and grow by the choices you make.

❖   Contemplate the fact that your Father in Heaven blocked out the memory of your pre-earth life so that you can learn to walk by faith, as you make decisions that will mold and shape your character.

❖   Ask your loving Heavenly Father to help you to again feel the closeness to Him that you once cherished.

Chapter 3

What Is My Purpose for Being Here on Earth?

❖   Make decisions throughout your life that will help you develop the kind of character that will feel comfortable in the presence of divine purity, kindness, and love.

❖   Learn to choose between opposing forces of good and evil by paying attention to the promptings and feelings that come from your internal moral compass known as your conscience.

❖   Find fulfillment in life by serving and loving God and your fellowman.

❖ Follow these four simple steps when you pray: Address your Heavenly Father, thank Him for your blessings, ask for the things you need, and end your prayers in the name of Jesus Christ.

❖ Pray by pouring out the feelings of your heart instead of relying on memorized prayers.

❖ Listen for answers to your prayers, which usually come in the form of feelings and impressions in your heart or thoughts that come into your mind.

❖ Feel free to pray any time of the day, whether you are driving down the road or kneeling beside your bed.

❖ Place a copy of the following saying on your bathroom mirror, refrigerator, or desk: *"If you have not first chosen the kingdom of God, it will in the end make no difference what you have chosen instead."*

Chapter 4

Do I Have to Experience Hardships and Difficulties?

❖ Understand that you will experience hardships, disappointments, frustration, pain, and discouragement as a part of the learning process of earth life.

❖ Reflect on the fact that the greatest opportunities for growth and progress come during times of struggle and pain.

❖ Select a positive attitude that will allow your times of suffering to build you, not destroy you.

❖ Take comfort in the fact that your Heavenly Father will not require you to bear any burden that is greater than you can bear.

❖ Dwell on the opportunities that are left for you in this life, not on the mistakes of the past.

❖ Understand that if all our prayers were immediately answered, we would not grow and progress in this life.

❖ Avoid needless worry, frustration, and tension by turning to your Heavenly Father for comfort.

Chapter 5

Can I Find Happiness?

❖ It does not matter how many trials we have in life, just how we handle them. It does not matter how long we live, just how we live.

❖ Realize that you determine whether or not you will be happy, as you decide what will play upon the stage of your mind.

❖ Focus your attention on the roses in life, not the thorns.

❖ Recognize that happiness is not about being free of trouble, turmoil, illness, or worries.

❖ Listen to good music.

❖ Maintain a sense of humor.

❖ Be courteous and kind.

❖ Take time to smell the roses

❖ Forget about yourself and serve others.

❖ Live in harmony with the laws of God and follow the promptings of your conscience.

❖ Remember it does not matter how many trials we have in life, just how we handle them, or how long we live just how we live.

Chapter 6

Do I Need A Savior?

❖ Recognize that Jesus Christ was the perfect role model who taught us how to live and then demonstrated his teachings by the way he lived.

❖ Ponder the fact that you have made mistakes that make you ineligible to return to your heavenly home without the assistance of a mediator or savior.

❖ Express gratitude to your Father in Heaven for sending Jesus Christ to serve as your Savior and pay for your sins and mine by enduring the most awful agony ever experienced by man.

❖ Contemplate the fact that Jesus Christ died while on the cross and returned to life three days later as a resurrected being.

❖ Realize that the Jesus Christ's sacrifice is the most important event in your life because.

   o He overcame death so that you will also overcome death and live forever.

   o He made it possible for you to be forgiven of your sins, which will enable you to return to live with your Heavenly Father *if* you do all that He has asked you to do.

   o Understand that, because of the sacrifice of the Savior, all the hardships, disappointments, illnesses, pains, and injustices you suffered in this life will be more than made up to you.

Chapter 7

What Happens When I Die?

❖ Realize that your kind and loving Heavenly Father sent you to earth to learn and to grow, and when your time on earth is over, you will die and begin the next stage of your existence.

❖ Understand that when death takes place,

- o Your physical body of flesh and bone is separated from your spirit body.

- o Your physical body that is made up of the elements returns to the earth.

- o Your spirit body that existed before you came to earth moves on to begin the next stage of progression.

- o Your spirit will first go to the world of spirits where you will have the chance to be reacquainted with many of your friends and loved ones who preceded you in death.

- o Your spirit body will no longer be subject to the pains, illnesses, or other infirmities that were associated with the physical body.

- o Your same character and personality that you possessed on earth will continue with you in the next stage of your life.

- o You will be assigned to paradise or prison in the spirit world, depending upon how you lived your life while on earth.

      o You will be taught about the teachings of Jesus Christ if you have not already accepted them.

❖ Realize that death is nothing to fear, as what could be more natural than a son or daughter returning home to their Father?

Chapter 8

What is the Resurrection and Judgment?

❖ Ponder the fact that no matter how good a life you live, and how many good deeds you perform, you cannot save yourself; you need your Savior's help.

❖ Realize that Jesus Christ was the first person to ever come forth from the grave as a resurrected being, never to die again, and opened the way for you to do the same.

❖ Understand that when you are resurrected your spirit and body will be reunited and you will inherit an immortal body that will never again be subject to pain, illness, disease, aging, or death.

❖ Recognize that the resurrection that was made possible by the Savior, is a free gift which is given to you and **everyone** else who will live on the earth.

❖ Understand that you will be judged on the content of your character, which is developed during your lifetime by the things you do and by your thoughts and feelings.

❖ Live the commandments that the Savior has given you, and his sacrifice will pay for your sins and he will stand as your advocate on the day of judgment.

❖ Anticipate that you will receive as an inheritance, a kingdom of glory that will reflect how you have lived your life and followed the teachings of Jesus Christ.

❖ Express gratitude to your loving Father in Heaven for His beautiful plan of salvation, which provides the opportunity for you to be able to return to live with Him and share a never-ending, glorious life of peace and joy.

REFERENCES

All Biblical citations are from the King James Version of the Holy Bible.

CHAPTER ONE
1.1   Genesis 1:26-27.
1.2   Acts 17:23, 24, 27, 28
1.3   Matthew 6: 26, 28-30
1.4   Psalm 8:3-5
1.5   Matthew 7: 7-11

CHAPTER TWO
2.1   Jeremiah 1:4-6.
2.2   Ephesians 1:4
2.3   Timothy 1: 9
2.4   Job 38:7
2.5   Luke 2:13-14

CHAPTER THREE

3.1   Revelation 12:7-9
3.2   John 8: 7, 9
3.3   John 8:31-32
3.4   Matthew 22: 37-39
3.5   Matthew 10:22
3.6   Genesis 39:21, 23
3.7   Genesis 41:38-40
3.8   Matthew 25:34
3.9   Mark 11: 24
3.10 James 1: 5

CHAPTER FOUR

4.1   Genesis 3:17,18,19
4.2   Revelations 3:19, 21
4.3   Hebrews 5:8
4.4   1 Corinthians 10:13
4.5   Proverbs 3:11-12
4.6   Proverbs 3:5-7
4.7   Philippians 4:7
4.8   Psalms 46:1, 3, 10
4.9   2 Corinthians 12:9
4.10 2 Corinthians 12:9, 10

CHAPTER FIVE
5.1   Psalms 118:24
5.2   1 Samuel 16: 23

CHAPTER SIX
6.1   Romans 3:23
6.2   Luke 22:44
6.3   John 19:30
6.4   Luke 23:46
6.5   John 20:11-16
6.6   Matthew 27:52-53
6.7   1 Corinthians 15:22
6.8   John 10:18
6.9   Luke 22:42
6.10   John 14:15
6.11   Acts 9:6
6.12   Matthew 8:17
6.13   Luke 2:10

CHAPTER SEVEN

7.1   Psalms 104:29
7.2   Luke 8:41-42, 49-55
7.3   James 2:26
7.4   Ecclesiastes 12:7
7.5   1 Peter 3: 18-19
7.6   1 Peter 4:6
7.7   John 5:25
7.8   Luke 16:19-26

CHAPTER EIGHT

8.1   Matthew 28:6
8.2   Luke 24:36-40
8.3   Luke 24: 41-43
8.4   1 Corinthians 15:20-22
8.5   Isaiah 25:8
8.6   1 Corinthians 15:55
8.7   Matthew 27:52-53
8.8   1 Corinthians 15:23, 25-26
8.9   1 Thessalonians 4:14, 16-17
8.10   Revelation 20: 4-5
8.11   Daniel 12:2
8.12   John 5:28-29
8.13   Malachi 3:5
8.14   Ecclesiastes 12:13-14
8.15   Matthew 12:36
8.16   Revelation 20:12
8.17   Matthew 25:40
8.18   John 14:2

Please Write to Me

If you have questions that were not answered in this book, or if you would like to share your thoughts or experiences, please write to me at:

Phil Batchelor
PO Box 3213
Danville CA 94526

Or email to: Phil@planofhappiness.net

The Danville Int'l Publishing Company's books are available at quantity discounts for sales promotions, premiums, or fund raising.

For information, write to

Danville Int'l Publishing Co., LLC
PO Box 3213
Danville, CA 94526.

ABOUT THE AUTHOR

Phil Batchelor is the author of "Raising Parents, Nine Powerful Principles" which was a very successful book on parenting. It received the unique distinction of being ordered by a California school district for distribution to parents of the students in the district. After the second printing, St Martin's Press published another edition under the title "Love is a Verb".

Phil is a devoted husband and father. He has had many teaching opportunities throughout his life and has worked extensively with young people. He served for many years as the Chair of the Children and Family Forum in his home county and was appointed by the Governor of California to sit on the committee of the California Youth Forum.

He has been an avid student of the scriptures for over forty years and is currently working on other books, including one on prayer and another on the attributes of Jesus Christ. He has learned that we can know who we really are, why we are here on earth, and what lies ahead once we have completed our journey in this life.

ORDER FORM

If you would like to order additional copies of this book to share with a friend or loved one, or you know someone who would like to more fully understand the purpose of life, or is facing challenges, send a check or money order made out to "Purpose of Life" and mail to:

**Purpose of Life
PO Box 3213
Danville CA 94256**

Please send me _____ copy/copies of the Purpose of Life for $12.95 plus $3.00 for shipping and handling (Total $15.95* US each).

{ } Check enclosed { } Visa { } Master Card { } Discover Card

Name as it appears on card _____

Credit Card No ._____

Exp. Date (mo/year) _____

Phone Number (_____)_____

Address line 1 _____

Address line 2 _____

City _____ State____ Zip code _____

Signature _____

Ship To:

Name _____

Address line 1 _____

Address line 2 _____

City _____ State____ Zip Code _____

* Discounts available online at: www.planofhappiness.net.